THE IOWA FLOODS OF 2008

One Week in June

WDG Publishing

THE IOWA FLOODS OF 2008

One Week in June

Jeff Stein

Published by WDG Publishing

The Iowa Floods of 2008
One Week in June

Editor: Elinor Day, Sher Jasperse
Design/Art Direction/Production: Duane Wood, Jodi Hormann, Eric Johnson

First published in the United States of America by
WDG Communications Inc.
1615 32nd Street NE
Suite Two
Cedar Rapids, Iowa 52402-4072
Telephone (319) 396-1401
Facsimile (319) 396-1647

Library of Congress Cataloging in Publication record is on file.

ISBN: 978-0-9793779-8-3

Printed in the United States of America
by Cedar Graphics, Inc., Hiawatha, Iowa.

10 9 8 7 6 5 4 3 2 1

Contents

I was afraid to answer the phone when I saw who was calling. Of course, I had also been afraid to make that call myself. What do you say?

It was about a week after the Cedar River had crested in Cedar Rapids. Like thousands of Iowans, I watched with horror as the devastation of the Iowa floods of 2008 played out on my television screen. When I saw the first video of downtown Cedar Rapids, and saw the river raging through the first floor of the Hach Building, I exclaimed out loud, even though no one else was in the room.

The Hach Building was home to WDG Communications Inc., the company operated by Duane and JoAnn Wood. We worked closely together and became friends during the two-and-one-half-year process leading to their publication of my book, *Making Waves: The People and Places of Iowa Broadcasting.* Now, like so many other businesses throughout Iowa, what once had been a thriving office was full of angry, rushing river water. Their new downtown office, which they had all taken such pride in decorating, was ruined.

It was Woody on the phone, calling to let me know what had happened to WDG Communications. He told of moving computers and hard drives out of the office, of taking client materials and manuscripts off-site, just to be safe. He described how everyone in the building pitched in to move material from the vulnerable first floor to what was thought to be safe quarters on the second floor — chairs, books, anything that could easily be carried up a flight of stairs. He told me of moving cases of inventory — books they had published but had yet to be distributed to booksellers — up to higher ground from the basement storage cages.

JoAnn Wood

Above: The Hach Building, 401 First Street SE, Cedar Rapids, Iowa. WDG Communications had over 8 feet of water in their first floor offices.

Opposite: In the early evening of Wednesday, June 11, 2008 pumps forced rising waters back over the flood wall along First Street SE in downtown Cedar Rapids, Iowa.

JoAnn Wood

And he described the sick feeling of helplessness when he saw the same images on television I did, of a river smashing through the plate glass windows of what used to be their office. At that point, they had not yet been able to enter the building, even the upper floors, to retrieve the things they had saved; the structure was not safe enough to reenter.

Then came the question I had been afraid to ask, the reason I was afraid to call to begin with: what now?

It would be easy to simply take Mother Nature's hint and call an end to this chapter of one's life. But his response was immediate.

"We find a place to set up our computers and get back to business," he said.

That scene was repeated in dozens of cities along Iowa's rivers during the amazing destruction of the floods of 2008. While it is a story of tremendous devastation and helplessness, as everything people had worked for was washed away, it is actually more a story of resilience, resolve, and rebirth.

In many ways, this is a uniquely Iowa story. The Iowa Floods of 2008 have often been called "Iowa's Katrina," a reference to the hurricane that struck this country's Gulf Coast in 2005. The chaos that ensued after that catastrophe remains etched in our minds, and the phrase "recovery" has hardly been uttered even to this day in many areas of that region.

But not here. We Iowans did what we always do — band together, help each other out, and spend our time fixing the problem instead of complaining that it

happened to us. Given our track record, that's not surprising.

It's part of the great Midwestern work ethic that makes us unique. When a storm leads to a tree falling, the rain has barely stopped before we hear the hum of chainsaws to clean up the mess. There's no time to sit around and whine about our plight; rather, it's time to roll up our sleeves and solve the problem.

It's why when tragedy or death strikes a family, you know your neighbors will be there with a plate of brownies or a casserole, along with sincere concern.

And it's why thousands of people volunteered to sandbag in a valiant effort to ward off greater devastation from a force we had never seen before — river levels twice flood stage in some places.

As an author, I would like to tell you to pay close attention to every word I have written that appears in this book. But honestly, no words I could write can adequately sum up what we went through as a people that One Week in June. However, the amazing, sometimes disturbing, photos in this book tell the story far better than any wordsmith could ever hope to do.

I had planned to tell you in this book the unique stories of what happened at each point where the river made its presence known. But in many places, that proved to be difficult, not because there were not local heroes at every stage, but rather because no one thought what they did was special. When I would ask people about the endless supply of sandbaggers of all ages, sizes and incomes who showed up on a moment's

JoAnn Wood

Above: With water already filling the streets, volunteers fill sandbags in the early evening of June 11 along First Street in downtown Cedar Rapids, Iowa.

Opposite: A drawing board lamp hangs out the broken window of the first floor offices of WDG Communications Inc. in Cedar Rapids, Iowa on Sunday, June 15, 2008. The high water mark is still visible on the side of the building.

JoAnn Wood

Above: The scene after the floodwaters receded from the WDG Communications Inc. offices in the Hach Building, Cedar Rapids, Iowa.

Opposite: Destruction left by flood water as it breached the window in the WDG Communications Inc. offices in the Hach Building, Cedar Rapids, Iowa.

The coffee mugs on the window sill remained there throughout the window breach and the torrent of water that flowed through.

notice when summoned, I would get in return a puzzled look, as if to say, "Well, what did you expect? Of course, that's what people would do."

Upon reflection, I guess that makes sense. My wife and I don't live on the river anymore, but we spent a day sandbagging at our former house, and spent other days helping former neighbors haul debris out of their ruined basements. We appreciated the help when the river hit then-record levels nearly a decade before, and it seemed wrong not to participate in protecting our community.

For some, that One Week in June was an exhilarating time they will not soon forget. Others, however, are still recovering from the effects a year after the waters flowed. They are rebuilding their businesses, rebuilding their homes, and rebuilding their lives.

The devastation was only one week in the making, but in many cases the recovery will take years.

Speaking of recovery, the publishers of this book quickly found temporary quarters and barely missed a beat in serving their clients across the country. Now in a new, permanent location, they are busy with new projects, really as if nothing had ever happened.

Obviously, something did happen, though, and it seems only fitting that such a book is produced by a company that survived the flood waters and is thriving today. In a lot of ways, that's the perfect metaphor for that whole One Week in June.

I thank them for the chance to be a part of this project. And to those affected by the Iowa Floods of 2008, I hope this book in some small way does justice to your experience.

Jeff Stein

Mike Schlotterback/Schlotterback Photographics

Mark Wicks/Charles City Press

Monday, June 9, 2008

Water Over the Dam

Mary Pieper/Globe Gazette

When citizens of Charles City awoke on Monday morning, something was missing.

The night before, the town's century-old, historic suspension bridge was swept away by flood waters.

The bridge had seen a lot since it was erected in 1906. It was a popular spot for sightseers, and even marriage proposals. In more recent times, it survived the deadly 1968 tornado, the 40th anniversary of which was commemorated less than a month before. Record flooding in 1993 and 1999 failed to shake it from its moorings. And in 2007, the city had spent nearly $190,000 to strengthen the structure.

Now, all that was left was a single bridge support.

The Cedar River crested at 25.55 feet in Charles City shortly before noon Monday — nearly three feet above the 1999 record, and more than twice the flood stage of 12 feet.

Folks knew it was coming, of course. That same morning, north in St. Ansgar, the overflowing Cedar spilled into smaller streams, causing two thirds of homeowners in that town to have either flooded or damaged basements. And the night before, the Winnebago River at Mason City crested at 18.74 feet, far above the flood stage of seven feet and nearly four feet above the top of the city's levee. Hundreds were evacuated, and the city was without drinking water for five days.

But the bridge? Even those who said they expected it to collapse some day were not ready for the shock of looking out and seeing an empty space where that symbol of the city once stood.

As the water crested Monday, no one could anticipate that a second crest would soon be on its way, thanks to heavy rains that would fall in the region on Wednesday. Cleanup from the record flood was underway as the second crest hit Saturday night, the eighth highest river level in history in Charles City. By comparison, Saturday's flood-to-come would not seem so bad.

More than 100 people were evacuated before the initial crest, typically hanging a white towel or sheet on the door handle as they left, to assist emergency personnel in any rescue efforts.

Top: Julie Begemann (right) and her daughter, Lauren Begemann, 19, were among the volunteers filling sandbags at the Hy-Vee parking lot in Charles City Thursday.

Opposite: The bridge wreckage is what is left of Charles City's historic Suspension Bridge, which was swept under by flood waters on the Cedar River at 11 p.m. June 8, 2008.

6/9
Cedar River crested
on this date in 2008.

12.00 ft.
Flood stage

22.81 ft.
Flood crest recorded in 1999

25.55 ft.
Flood crest on June 9, 2008

2.74 ft.
Higher flood crest than
previous record in 1999

Charles City, Iowa

Photograph Cresco Times
National Weather Service Data

Arian Schuessler /The Globe Gazette

Mike Munshower/The Globe Gazette

Left: The Cedar River cascades over a then-nonessential Main Street dam and under the Main Street Bridge in Charles City.

Below left & right: Volunteers turned out in droves the night of June 8 to fill sandbags in Charles City as the Cedar River rose faster than forecasted. The county's supply of sandbags was exhausted by the next day and additional sandbags had to be trucked in.

Opposite: The Brantingham Bridge in Charles City on June 9, 2008. The flooded Cedar Terrace senior-housing complex is at the top. The Immaculate Conception Catholic Church remains an island at right .

Mark Wicks/Charles City Press

Mark Wicks/Charles City Press

Above: Many of the businesses along South Grand Avenue in Charles City were affected by the flood waters of the Cedar River.

Right: The Charles City McDonald's® restaurant is flooded, along with many other businesses along South Grand Avenue.

Far Right: Water rages under the Main Street Bridge, Charles City, Iowa.

That universal symbol of surrender is not usually in the vocabulary of citizens in America's Hometown — but this was not a normal time. Around 1,000 homes in Floyd County were directly impacted as Day One came to a close.

It was a very long year for residents of Charles City. The Memorial Day weekend tornado in Parkersburg was the strongest to hit the state since the devastating twister that struck Charles City 40 years before, leading painful memories to resurface. Then two of the greatest floods in the town's history hit in the same week. Just as the city was relaxing at an Independence Day celebration, a fireworks accident injured more than three dozen people who were watching Fourth of July fireworks along — yes, the river.

How, then, to heal? How can a community that lost such an iconic structure as the suspension bridge truly heal with that gaping hole in the city's landscape? In late October, the City Council voted in favor of replacing the historic bridge with a cable-stay bridge costing nearly $5 million. The old bridge could not be salvaged, nor could an identical bridge be made to meet modern construction requirements. Plans call

for adding aesthetic elements to help the new structure more closely resemble the old.

But to many citizens, it will never be the same.

Down river, Nashua stood as a town divided. The entire east side of the community was cut off by the overflowing river. A city water main running under the river broke, leaving the east side of town without drinkable water. Some three feet of water covered Iowa Highway 346.

Residents remembered the "great floods" of 1961, 1993 and 1999. Obviously, none would compare with 2008. On a normal day, the Cedar River falls 12 feet over the dam at Nashua. But at the crest Monday afternoon, the water was so high that the dam was not even visible.

Two dozen dump truck loads of sand were bagged by volunteers, saving the downtown from devastation. That hard work proved crucial on Monday, and later in the week during the second crest.

Nashua holds an annual community festival the last weekend of June, called "Water Over the Dam Days." In 2008, they learned for the first time what "water over the dam" really was like.

Mike Munshower/Mason City Globe Gazette

Above: Boat outside Immaculate Conception Catholic Church, corner of Clark and Brantingham St., Charles City, Iowa.

Tuesday, June 10, 2008

The River Ran Through It

Anelia K. Dimitrova/Waverly Newspapers

Above: A handmade sign urges volunteers to sign in to help sandbag.

Opposite: Flood waters rise in Waverly, Iowa, on Tuesday, June 10, 2008.

Jim Ostman looked out the second floor window of his house as the sun rose Tuesday morning. The Cedar River was normally 200 feet from his back door, down a sloping backyard. Now, it was only ten feet away, with nothing but a five-foot-high sandbag wall keeping it from coming in.

But that wasn't the big problem.

The big problem was the water about to enter the front of the Ostman house. Never before had the river jumped its banks and spilled that far down First Street SE in Waverly. Literally, his house was on an island, and with the crest still a few hours off, the water was just inches from coming in the front door like an unwelcome guest.

His wife Sheri and their children had obeyed the evacuation order issued by the city and left the night before. Jim stayed behind and called her early that morning with the news: the basement was full, and it was close to coming onto the main floor. They'd moved to the house 20 months before, and had never before experienced a flood.

While Jim's mind was on what would happen to his family's home, he was also thinking about the flood's effect on other properties — their former home, which was now rented to another family; another home they owned, where Sheri's son was living; a storage garage he rented in nearby Shell Rock, where the Shell Rock River was cresting at a record level — all those properties, taking on water as the force of the flood hit.

The day before, while friends, neighbors and volunteers built walls to hold the river off from the back of the houses, an evacuation was taking place.

Not of people, but animals.

Sheri Ostman operates the nonprofit Waverly Pet Rescue from the family's home. A dozen cats — already without a permanent place to call home — were now being moved to safety in the back of a truck by a volunteer. Their own pets were evacuated, too.

By Tuesday morning, the now-empty cages in the cat shelter awaited the midday crest.

When the river is adjacent to your backyard, you know you may be at risk for flooding. But when you live where you cannot even see the river, you think you're safe. Not when the Cedar raged throughout this Bremer County town of 9,000 in 2008. The Cedar

6/10
Cedar River crested
on this date in 2008

11.5 ft.
Flood stage

16.8 ft.
Flood crest recorded in 1999

19.12 ft.
Flood crest on June 10, 2008

2.32 ft.
Higher flood crest than
previous record in 1999

Waverly, Iowa

Photograph Angela Worrell.
National Weather Service Data

Anelia K. Dimitrova/Waverly Newspapers

Clint Riese/Waverly Newspapers

Clint Riese/Waverly Newspapers

Above Top: On Monday, June 9, David Kelly and a group of friends came to help the Riggs family at 500 First St. SE, which borders the Cedar River. Some 200,000 sandbags were used in Waverly.

Above Bottom: Wartburg students Britney Stensland, Ashley Steines and Marissa Kinseth volunteered to fill bags for others at St. Paul's Lutheran Church, even while they worried about getting cut off from their home near Cedar Lane.

poured over its banks, filling an 11-block-wide area in the heart of the city. The main connection between the east and west halves of the town, the Bremer Avenue bridge on Iowa Highway 3, was closed for two days.

The historic Post Office, built with WPA funding in the 1930s and located a block from the river, would close, not to reopen for eight months. One downtown restaurant was closed for more than a month because of water in the basement of its building; even though the water never reached the dining level, state officials would not approve reopening the restaurant until all water was out of the structure. City Hall, which

overlooks the river, was flooded and city offices operated for months out of temporary quarters at the Waverly Public Library on the west side of the river.

Washington Irving Elementary School was inundated with flood waters, and was later deemed forever unusable as a school. Southeast Elementary classrooms had as much as four feet of water in them, which sounds like a lot — until one considers that the junior high gymnasium was filled with 20 feet of water at one point.

Residents south of the city's downtown dam were not only flooded, they felt betrayed. They relied on city

Anelia K. Dimitrova/Waverly Newspapers

projections that indicated the water would not reach them, and were shocked to find basements full of tainted flood water and ruined property. Their shock quickly turned to anger when they learned that the city knew the earlier public projections were too low — by about three feet — but did not publicly revise them until the morning of the crest, when it was too late for citizens to protect their property. Monday afternoon, city officials ordered evacuation of homes along the river — approximately a quarter of the town — and publicly projected a crest below the 1999 record.

By Tuesday morning, the revised projections told

a vastly different story.

At the time, Waverly did not have an official National Weather Service hydrological reporting station, meaning citizens had only one source for information about possible river levels — the city. Rumors were passed along sandbag lines Monday about the Charles City bridge collapse. Some said they heard it was the river dam itself that collapsed, which caused a more furious pace of sandbagging for a time.

The Tuesday midday crest of 19.12 feet was 7.5 feet above flood stage and almost 2.5 feet above 1999's record. About 1,000 Waverly homes and businesses

Above: The waters breached the broken railroad tracks in New Hartford, where the flood was the second disaster to hit in just over two weeks. On May 25, an EF-5 tornado ripped through the north edge of town.

Opposite Right: Most of the flood waters had receded by Wednesday morning, but not north of Bremer Avenue around City Hall. Rain added to the muck as home and business owners pumped water and carried valuables out of their homes and offices.

Top: The Flaig family of 304 Sixth St. NW tried to keep spirits high as water approached their front door. Dad Clint made several trips across the street to bring more valuables to the top floor. On later river crossings, he wore a life preserver as he sought to save the family's movie collection and a cane rocker that belonged to his wife's great-great-grandmother. The family had only found one of their four cats, and Clint and wife Melissa assured their son, Braden, that his turtles would survive because they could swim.

Bottom: An adventure seeker tests the waters in the middle of Bremer Avenue on Tuesday, June 10. The water carried to the 800 block of the west side of the river.

were without power Tuesday afternoon. The next Sunday morning, another crest would come, this one the fourth highest level in recorded history. Because of that, the city suspended cleanup operations for a time after the initial crest, fearful that the second crest would create a more hazardous situation as curbside debris was carried off by new flood waters.

The breakdown of trust between the citizens and their government came to a head at a city council meeting less than a week after the flood waters first crested. Officials indicated they did not sound a siren or revise public statements about the expected river level because they did not want to cause panic. More than one citizen said they would have preferred a brief panic as opposed to being unaware of the extent of the flood waters and not having a chance to protect their property — or perhaps drowning because they had stayed in their homes, believing they were safe.

Waverly's town-and-gown relationship with Wartburg College was further cemented during the emergency. The college's recreation center became a Red Cross shelter, and dormitory space was utilized as temporary housing for those displaced by the flood.

The campus Center for Community Engagement became the official headquarters for the city's flood recovery relief and coordination of volunteer efforts.

But in their frustration, some residents were not satisfied by these efforts. They noted that the emergency headquarters were on the west side of the river and therefore inaccessible to those who were on the east side, because all bridges within the city had been closed — an omission city officials later recognized and pledged to remedy in future

emergencies. Some also criticized the fact that the college charged a small fee for some of its housing, while others thought that "coordination of volunteers" meant there was a pool of able bodies waiting to spring into action, and did not immediately understand that there was a waiting list, depending on how many people actually volunteered on a given day.

Just south of Waverly, in Janesville, the water was so high that the hydrological service river gauge stopped working, leading to an even greater information blackout for citizens; later in the week, the same fate would befall the gauge in Cedar Rapids. Ultimately, the river crested Tuesday evening at 19.7 feet, almost nine feet above flood stage. South of Janesville, officials evacuated four people by boat, including an 18-month-old baby. Other evacuees were transported by a Janesville school district bus. The Janesville Fire Department was unable to access some portions of the fire district. As the river made its way to its next target, the metro areas of Cedar Falls and Waterloo, it appeared to actually be rising, if the recorded levels in Waverly and Janesville were any indication.

In the spring, a new business had opened in downtown Waverly one block west of the river. The city had not had a pet store for almost ten years before Noah's Ark opened in a former building supply store. The flooding overwhelmed that portion of Waverly's downtown, and while the store reopened for a time after the flood, it soon had a "going out of business" sale.

Even Noah's Ark was no match for the Cedar River in this year.

Anelia K. Dimitrova/Cedar Falls Times

Wednesday, June 11, 2008

Washed Away

Anelia K. Dimitrova/Cedar Falls Times

Many in Cedar Falls breathed a sigh of relief as midnight turned Tuesday into Wednesday.

The downtown just might be safe, after all.

The crest came a few minutes before midnight, at 102.13 feet. At 103 feet, water would have begun spilling over the earthen levy that protects that part of the city from the Cedar River.

It doesn't get much closer than that.

The levee was constructed to be 15 feet higher than flood stage. All the previous top-ten flood levels had been between 94 and 96 feet, including 1999's record of 96.20 feet.

In 2008, it almost wasn't enough to protect the downtown. But while some were celebrating victory, others not far to the north were already devastated by the river's impact.

Residents of the North Cedar neighborhood had been warned by city officials on Sunday to leave before the waters rose. Then the city expanded its warning zone. And then expanded it once again.

Rescue operations were conducted Monday and Tuesday for those residents who didn't believe the water would rise that far, that fast. Later, some blamed the focus on saving the downtown with actually

causing them more damage; while the levee protects the Parkade downtown, it restricts the flood plain on that side of the river, pushing water into northern Cedar Falls neighborhoods. In reality, the crush of the unprecedented amount of water that came so fast led officials to believe — correctly, as it turned out — that no amount of sandbagging would have saved the North Cedar area; some termed even trying to be a "lost cause." Nearly 600 homes in North Cedar Falls were under water, with half of those seeing water onto the first floor.

And there was never a certainty that the downtown would be spared either. As more rain fell in the region, and the projections of flood crest rose, an army of sandbaggers turned out to shore up the downtown levee and add some height where needed.

Some 4,000 volunteers — from area residents to college students — worked round-the-clock in waves, filling extra bags in case a "soft spot" developed in the mile-long earthen wall separating the heart of a city from a torrent of water.

When the call went out Monday and Tuesday for volunteers, the response was overwhelming. Those lending aid were asked to report to the UNI Dome on the south end of the city to be bussed in, to lessen the

Above: The community teamed up for an historic sandbag effort that kept the Cedar River from taking over downtown.

Opposite: A 5-foot mountain of sandbags reinforcing the wall along the trail separates the swelling river from the town.

6/11
Cedar River crested
on this date in 2008

88.00 ft.
Flood stage

96.20 ft.
Flood crest recorded in 1999

102.13 ft.
Flood crest on June 11, 2008

5.93 ft.
Higher flood crest than
previous record in 1999

Cedar Falls, Iowa

Photograph Anelia K. Dimitrova, Cedar Falls Times
National Weather Service Data

Matthew Putney/Courier Photo Editor

Left: Flood waters rise in Cedar Falls, Iowa, Tuesday, June 10, 2008.

Opposite:

Top: After the volunteers went home, the sandbags looked like wildflowers against the backdrop of the rising water.

Bottom left: The community teamed up for an historic sandbag effort that kept the Cedar River from taking over downtown.

Bottom center: On the other side of the road, the effort to contain the rising water was just as intense.

Bottom right: Jared Rickard, 10, and Jordan Bearbower, 10, came with Jared's mom Twyla, who owns Custom Image Embroidery. "We wanted them to see how the community comes together," she said. Added Jared, "It's a little too close for comfort."

David Beck

traffic load in a downtown area that had been ordered closed and otherwise evacuated earlier.

Television station KWWL, the local NBC affiliate based in Waterloo-Cedar Falls, provided live coverage from the heart of the sandbagging effort during its extended newscasts, and local officials used the opportunity not only to keep citizens informed, but to issue those calls for help.

Veteran anchor Ron Steele was among those who reported live from the scene on Tuesday, and later noted that one of the early clues to how monumental the flooding would be was the fact that rising waters in both cities made it nearly impossible for the television crew to get from the station in downtown Waterloo over to the Parkade area of downtown Cedar Falls due to road closures.

In the end, the weight of the sandbag wall on the earthen levee kept it from eroding away. The bags would be needed again a few days later, as the second crest of the Cedar River struck, nearly seven feet above the normal flood stage. The bags remained in place, weeks after the flooding — just in case. They stood in defiant reminder of the water's presence, as did the crumpled metal fences along roadways in that area, laden with debris, pushed and bent by the Cedar's force. The distorted fences remained a year later.

Levees were a concern in Waterloo, as well. The levee system there was built in the 1970s to withstand up to 28 feet of flood water, more than five feet above the 1961 record levels.

By Tuesday morning, though, while the levees were holding, no fewer than five city bridges over the Cedar were closed as a precaution, and Mayor

Tim Hurley ordered downtown businesses to shut their doors, as well. Riverfront Stadium was already under water, and would be closed for much of the summer.

But while downtown Waterloo readied for the crest, residents of the Sans Souci Island area were already getting water in their homes. Despite the efforts of dozens who were sandbagging the east side of the island, a sandbag dike gave way at 9:30 p.m. Monday night, and officials advised evacuation of the area, a neighborhood of private homes that is prone to flooding, but where long-time residents are resolute in their desire to remain no matter how many times a year the island takes on water. They call it a "sanctuary" that is worth living with the yearly flooding risk. After 2008's record flooding, and basements in some homes collapsing, rendering those homes unsafe, some reconsidered that position.

The Cedar's crest in Waterloo was still nearly a day away when a sickening cracking sound was heard. About one-third of a railroad bridge crossing the river in Waterloo was swept away by the river shortly before 3 p.m. Tuesday afternoon. The bridge was used to transport tractors from the John Deere Tractor Works to Cedar Rapids.

The structure creaked, the rails popped up in the air, and the section adjacent to the Cedar's east bank slipped away, slamming into the city's 18th Street bridge downstream. Part of the rail bridge continued its path down the river, while part remained lodged for a time against the 18th Street bridge, almost as a suggestion of further damage to come.

By late afternoon Tuesday, business owners were concerned about the river spilling over a flood wall.

Cedar Falls Times

Above: The waters nearly invaded this mailbox.

Opposite: A geiser-effect is caused by water forced from a manhole on Tuesday, June 10, 2008.

Opposite, Clockwise:
The Ice House Museum is
surrounded by flood waters
on Tuesday, June 10, 2008
in Cedar Falls, Iowa.

Television crews
set up outside The Ice House
Museum, Cedar Falls, Iowa,
to broadcast the disaster
news to a national audience.

Hundreds of items lay in ruin
outside the Ice House Museum,
Cedar Falls, Iowa.

Waters rise around
The Ice House Museum.

The saturated ground led to groundwater seeping into downtown buildings as early as Monday — two days before the actual high water mark of the river itself.

In the end, the river mainly stayed in its banks and moved along to its next target. But that did not mean Waterloo was dry.

A further mandatory evacuation and overnight curfew was ordered Wednesday, after the crest, because the city's lift stations in the area were not able to keep up with groundwater runoff — not river water, or levee breaches, but groundwater.

Storm drainage problems downtown led to water spewing up through manhole covers, flooding streets that were blocks away from the river itself and were not protected by sandbags. Some downtown businesses saw up to three feet of water slap against their buildings. In downtown Waterloo, more damage was caused by that than by the Cedar itself.

In times of crisis, people crave information. The Cedar River flooding spared no one, not even those who were charged with providing news and information to the public.

The Community Newspapers Group saw two of its publications affected immediately. The offices of the Waverly Democrat and Bremer County Independent in downtown Waverly sit only three blocks from the river and were quickly overcome by water. The Cedar Falls Times' downtown office was also evacuated, with groundwater coming into the basement.

The papers didn't miss an issue, thanks to the staff gathering a makeshift collection of computers and equipment and setting up shop in the Cedar Falls home of editor Anelia Dimitrova.

The Waterloo-Cedar Falls Courier not only covered the story, but also coped with the paper's headquarters becoming an island, with water on all sides. Phone service to the newspaper was also disrupted.

Just after the crest Wednesday afternoon, the Courier newsroom moved to space at Hawkeye Community College in Waterloo. The paper was written and designed there, sent to Cedar Rapids for printing, and distributed back in Waterloo — no easy feat, given that the normal transportation routes were closed due to flood water.

The need for immediate information during a crisis leads many to turn to radio and television stations for the most current warnings and details. But the waters rendered many local broadcasting outlets silent during a key point in the Waterloo flooding.

The flood waters knocked out a downtown Waterloo power substation Wednesday morning as the waters crested, preventing KWWL-TV from broadcasting for more than three hours. By mid-morning, the station was back on the air, using a back-up generator with anchors reporting from a makeshift location in the station's parking lot.

Three radio stations located in the Black's building downtown suffered a similar fate, and were forced from the air due to the same power outage. Phones also were not working, so staffers were unable to tell people why they were off the air.

In the end, Waterloo saw a record crest of 25.39 feet Wednesday, more than 3.5 feet above the 47-year-old record level, and more than double the flood stage downtown of 12 feet.

Two days later, city crews and volunteers were still working to resolve problems caused by 'hot spots' popping up behind the levee system. Pumps were still

This Page: Cedar Falls Historical Society

6/11
Cedar River crested
on this date in 2008

12.00 ft.
Flood stage

21.86 ft.
Flood crest recorded in 1961

25.39 ft.
Flood crest on
June 11, 2008

3.53 ft.
Higher flood crest than
previous record in 1961

Waterloo, Iowa

Photograph David Beck
National Weather Service Data

David Beck

Above: A railroad bridge is destroyed by the raging water in Waterloo.

humming, and sandbags were still being filled, as the river was again on the rise toward a second, weekend crest. In between the two crests, citizens assessed the damage. There was much to assess.

While Cedar Falls Utilities was able to maintain service to customers, CFU's downtown power plant was out of commission for six months; the utility was out of its administrative offices for longer than that.

The Ice House Museum in Cedar Falls took a direct hit from the flood of 2008. A six-foot-high wall of sandbags was simply not enough. Water spilled over the top of the bags, and the building interior was overcome by five feet of water. The water ultimately rose so high it nearly touched the canopy over the museum entrance. The pre-flood efforts focused on sandbagging, rather than removal of items, so the

David Beck

water had plenty of things to touch once it entered the historic structure.

Ironically, much of the loss there was limited by the nature of the Ice House itself; since it is not a climate-controlled structure, only items that could endure extremes were stored there, as opposed to photographs or books.

Some wood items were destroyed, others merely warped. Glass and metal items needed a good cleaning, provided by teams of volunteers.

A year later, the Ice House Museum was still "closed until further notice due to flood damage."

Across the way, another fixture of the northern part of downtown Cedar Falls was not as lucky. When the waters receded, the historic Island Park Beach House, a fixture along the Cedar since 1920, was

Above: Water swiftly runs below the Fourth Street Bridge, Waterloo, Iowa

Anelia K. Dimitrova, Cedar Falls Times

Orlan Love/The Gazette

Matthew Putney/Courier Photo Editor

Scott Mussell/Courier

Anelia K. Dimitrova/Cedar Falls Times

Clockwise:
Lives, like bare nerves, lay open on sidewalks and lawns in North Cedar.

Rushing floodwaters of the Cedar River nearly fill the first floors of homes on Sans Souci Island in Waterloo. Between 40 and 50 residents of the island in the Cedar River were forced to flee their homes Monday when a record flood filled them with water.

John Vos has lived at 142 N. Main since 1996 with his wife Susan Nieman. On Saturday, he returned to his flooded home to retrieve possessions. John and Susan's house got water up to its roofline.

An Iowa Army National Guard humvee makes its way Wednesday afternoon along Jefferson Street in Waterloo.

Secretary of Homeland Security Michael Chertoff speaks to media on the Mullan Ave Bridge Thursday, June 12, 2008 in Waterloo, Iowa.

Dennis Magee / Waterloo-Cedar Falls Courier

Rick Tibbott/Courier Staff Photographer.   Rick Tibbott/Courier Staff Photographer.   Rick Tibbott/Courier Staff Photographer

missing some walls which caved in due to the force of the water, and one end was sagging badly due to the lack of structural support. The river water had nearly reached the roofline of the structure, which was home to celebrations large and small for generations. The entire park was left littered with debris and literally tons of sand where green grass had once grown.

At the Waterloo Center for the Arts, workers and volunteers worked feverishly Tuesday to move the art collection from a basement storage area — an area that filled with groundwater the next day. About two feet of raw sewage filled another west side area. Damage to the new Phelps Youth Pavilion, which had just opened earlier in the spring, was minimal, and summer programming for children soon resumed there.

A few blocks away, a facility dedicated to one of Waterloo's native sons saw nearly a half-million dollars of damage.

The Dan Gable International Wrestling Institute and Museum had moved to Waterloo from Newton a year and a half before the flood. More than three-quarters of a million dollars was spent on renovation of a building, designed to anchor a downtown area of revitalization.

The museum was surrounded by flood waters on Tuesday night. Sandbagging prevented water from entering the building from the outside, but water backing up from the sewer system under the building devastated the first floor, which contained a large exhibit area. Nearly four feet of water filled the first floor, ruining carpeting, furniture and all 30 display cabinets. Gift shop inventory located in the basement, which included more than 15,000 items, was destroyed.

The museum had no flood insurance. Yet the facility was again up and running in time for the National Duals Wrestling Tournament held at the University of Northern Iowa, six months to the day from when the waters first entered the building.

Left: FEMA trailers in rows at the Greyhound Park grounds in Waterloo, Iowa, on Tuesday, June 12, 2008.

Bottom left: A statue remains untouched during the cleanup after a flood at the Dan Gable International Wrestling Institute and Museum on Tuesday, June 17, 2008 in Waterloo, Iowa.

Bottom right: Bruce Catchpool takes advantage of the free tetanus shots at North Cedar Elementary School in Cedar Falls, Iowa on Tuesday, June 17, 2008.

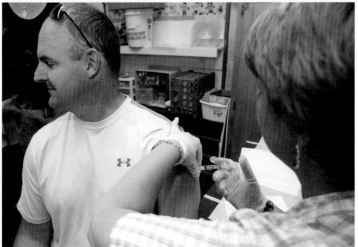

Thursday, June 12, 2008

Sandbags and Spirit

Once the waters topped off in Cedar Falls and Waterloo, many turned their attention to the next big target: Cedar Rapids.

But there would be a lot of destruction taking place in between.

Water started entering homes along the Cedar River outside La Porte City on Monday, and by the high water mark late Wednesday, several homes were submerged.

That was nothing new in 2008. Just after Memorial Day, heavy rains swelled Wolf Creek, causing it to rise six feet in a single afternoon, covering parts of Main Street and U.S. Highway 218. The same thing happened a week later.

Wolf Creek empties into the Cedar. But with the Cedar rising to record levels, there was nowhere for the overflow from the Wolf to go — except into homes and businesses. Now, the overflow caused the third soaking in a month, leaving mud-coated city streets in its wake — again.

Down river, the Benton County seat town of Vinton was experiencing the worst flooding in its history. Earlier projections that flooding would match the previous record, set in 1961, wound up being far short, thanks to another deluge of rain that fell early in the week.

Iowa Army National Guard members arrived Tuesday night to relieve volunteer sandbaggers. By then, sections of town had already been evacuated, and the previous record levels had already been reached. City intersections were already submerged, and the crest was still two days away.

Ultimately, flooding covered 15 blocks of the city along the river, and knocked out the municipal electrical generating plant. Generators were used to provide minimal power to the citizens, but it was only half what was normally produced.

It also led to evacuation of 30 inmates from the Benton County Jail on Wednesday. In a scene reminiscent of old-time chain gangs, prisoners dressed in black-and-white-striped jumpsuits were led to waiting school buses after being evacuated by boat from the jail itself to the nearby courthouse lawn.

Cedar Rapids television station KGAN-TV reported live from Vinton all day Thursday. Their cameras showed a solid line of sandbaggers, volunteers aged five to 75, working to save the jail building. The

Rick Tibbot/Courier Staff Photographer

Above: Jason Christensen (left) and Julia Christensen (center) carry six-month-olds Zigana Christensen and Meadow Chistensen from the La Porte City fire and rescue boat and the rising waters of the Cedar River as grandma Linda Sankey (right) releases the straps to the life jacket. Area fire and rescue departments worked through the day to rescue people from the rising Cedar River.

Opposite: Gwen Lewis (right) of Newhall moves a sandbag along a human chain to Jacob Hanson of Vinton as they and others work to protect a friend's home on Tuesday, June 10, 2008, in Vinton.

6/12
Cedar River crested
on this date in 2008

15.00 ft.
Flood stage

19.30 ft.
Flood crest recorded in 1961

24.60 ft.
Flood crest on June 12, 2008

5.30 ft.
Higher flood crest than
previous record in 1961

Vinton, Iowa

Top: Jocelyn Hanson of Vinton hefts a sandbag as part of a human chain and she and others work to protect a friend's home Tuesday, June 10, 2008, in Vinton.

Bottom: Vinton's Jessica Rippel's shadow is cast on a sandbag near the Benton County Sheriff's Office on Tuesday, June 10, 2008, in Vinton.

Above Right: Steve Johnson (left) of Vinton shovels sand into a bag held by Aegon employee Cristal (cq) Tanner of Marion as volunteers fill sandbags near the Benton County Sheriff's Office on Tuesday, June 10, 2008, in Vinton.

Opposite: Cattle were herded onto a porch and left to avoid drowning by the rising water from the Cedar River Wednesday, June 11, 2008 along the river north of Vinton, Iowa.

fire station and power plant — and most of the residences near the downtown area — were already beyond help.

Without power, the only sound heard was the hum of generators, an occasional motor boat with officials traveling on what used to be the street separating the jail from the courthouse — and a community pulling together.

It became a surreal, almost festive atmosphere, with citizens gathered on the courthouse lawn to help sandbag; businesses without power opting to donate food that could be cooked or grilled and served to volunteers, lest it otherwise go to waste; and above all, a glimmer of hope.

Businesses closed, as everyone came together to save what they could. Signs in the windows of business promoted the spirit, including one that read: "Closed. Sandbagging downtown. Why aren't you?"

"It was truly overwhelming to see all of these people sandbagging," said KGAN weathercaster Justin Roberts, who reported from the scene on Wednesday. "People who had already lost so much of their lives — yet here they are, helping to keep their neighbors from losing everything. This is what makes the Midwest great, Iowans being Iowans."

The crest came in Vinton on Thursday at 24.60 feet, nearly ten feet above flood stage and more than five feet above the old record. Nearly 100 homes were affected directly by the flooding.

A few hours before the high water mark, at 4 a.m., water breached a sandbag wall and flooded the Benton County Law Enforcement Building. The sheriff's office, communication center, and jail were termed a total loss at the time.

To add insult to injury, another five inches of rain soaked Benton County that morning. But as Friday dawned, the rain had stopped, the sun came out, and the river level had already dropped by a foot.

AP Photo/Steve Pope

Top: Nicole Williams (left to right), Tim Newnaber and Kevin Berry wait for a boat to pick them up from the front yard of Newnaber's parents home in Vinton on Thursday, June 12, 2008.

Bottom: Part of Lewis Bottoms Rd. was washed away by flood waters. Photographed Sunday, June 15, 2008, near Palo. Estimates for the repair of the washed-out road is around $500,000.

Above: Brian Geiger (left) of VanHorne and Lois Kray of Vinton check on a friend's home damaged by the high flood waters in Vinton on Thursday, June 12, 2008.

Jim Slosiarek/The Gazette

Above: Darrell Christy of Vinton works to clear a pump line of sand as he helps Ron Elwick (not pictured) clear water from around his son's home Tuesday, June 10, 2008, in Vinton.

6/13
Cedar River crested on this date in 2008

12.00 ft.
Flood stage

19.20 ft.
Flood crest recorded in 1993

31.12 ft.
Flood crest on June 13, 2008

11.92 ft.
Higher flood crest than previous record in 1993

Palo, Iowa

Photograph Liz Martin/The Gazette

Right: Sandbags are stockpiled by volunteers at the Palo Community Center in preparation for more flooding along the Cedar River on Tuesday, June 10, 2008.

Below Left: The flatbed truck rounds the corner of Iowa and Church Streets on its way to delivering sandbags Wednesday, June 11, 2008, in Palo.

Bottom Right: Iowa Governor Chet Culver thanks volunteers filling sand bags at the Palo Community Center in Palo on Tuesday, June 10, 2008. The governor met with Palo and Linn County officials to talk about flood preparations. He also visited Vinton and Iowa City.

Opposite:

Top: Merna Back (left) who lives near Lincoln and Linn Streets in Palo gets a hug from John Howerton pastor of the Palo United Methodist Church during a Palo town meeting at Atkins Elementary School on Sunday, June 15, 2008, in Atkins.

Bottom: Jennifer Cady of Palo looks out at her flooded backyard Wednesday, June 11, 2008, in Palo. Cady was staying with her grandmother in Covington until it was safe to come home.

Farther down the river, the town of Palo was fairly quiet Thursday morning. That's because officials had ordered a mandatory evacuation of the town's 890 residents the day before. Many of those who refused had to be rescued later, due to the fast-moving river and more rain that caused flash flooding.

Earlier in the week, city leaders worked with state officials to project various scenarios. They figured that if the river hit 20 feet, about half the town would be under water. If it reached 22 feet, then 80 percent would be under water.

Imagine how things looked when the actual crest — 31.12 feet — came on Friday morning, a dozen feet higher than it had ever reached before.

They knew it was coming, of course, so there was time to prepare. But how can you prepare for the entire town to be under water?

Residents who remembered the 1993 record flood tried to imagine what damage could be caused by even a few feet more of water. They took what they needed, thinking they'd be back in a day or so. For many, though, the return was a week away — and what they found was often staggering.

No matter. The spirit that only comes with living in a small town in Iowa would prevail. Spirit like that shown by 17-year-old Brooke Lentz.

A few days after the flooding, a letter arrived in Waverly. It was Brooke's application to be part of a July summer camp for high school students who wanted to learn about broadcasting at Wartburg College.

Those in charge of the camps were considering canceling the events because of the impact of the floods on so many Iowans; a workshop for high school teachers had already been canceled for that reason.

Brooke's application caught the organizers' attention because she listed two addresses with an arrow pointing to the back of the form, where she wrote, "Please send information to both addresses — we just got evacuated from Palo."

That was when it was decided the workshops would go on, no matter what; it would prove to be important for citizens across the state to have some sense of "normal" in the aftermath of the devastating week — if nothing else, as a break from the reality of cleanup, rebuilding, and starting over.

Prior to the flood, most knew Palo as the home of Iowa's only nuclear power plant, the Duane Arnold Energy Center. While that facility, built on the banks of the river, was not harmed, its primary communication source — landline phone service — was knocked out.

Through Father's Day weekend, the town itself was still off limits, due to road access being cut off. Debris and a swift current prevented any access in town by boat. Early the next week, some residents returned home for the first time in nearly a week to see what they had to deal with. Some were lucky enough to only find a flooded basement; others saw that the river had rushed through the first floor of their homes and businesses.

Nearly a year after the flood, most had returned to their homes, and the town was living up to its motto, "Growing Together."

But the river took a piece of everyone that week. And Cedar Rapids was next in line.

Jim Slosiarek/The Gazette

Jim Slosiarek/The Gazette

Tim Wilcox

Friday, June 13, 2008
Beyond Imagination

Cliff Jette/The Gazette

It was to be "The Year of the River."

More than a year before the Cedar River crushed Cedar Rapids, city and county leaders had decided to mark the centennial of the purchase of May's Island downtown, where the Cedar Rapids City Hall and Linn County Courthouse and law enforcement center were located, with a year-long effort to bring attention to the city's riverfront in hopes of stimulating private and public investment.

"The Year of the River" was designed to be a "rallying point of support" for the city's vision for the future of Cedar Rapids.

2008 would be remembered as "The Year of the River," alright.

The all-time highest level of the Cedar River in Cedar Rapids was originally seen in 1851. Certainly, no one who was there for that record was around in 2008. That record 20-foot level was also reached in 1929, but some 80 years later, not many could recall specifics, especially since so much had changed in Iowa's second largest city.

To be sure, the river rose and flooded areas of Cedar Rapids before — the "great floods" of 1961 and 1993 were close to the record, and incidents in 1965,

1999 and 2004 were all well above flood stage.

But to top the record of 20 feet? That's eight feet above flood stage. No one could imagine it.

Until it happened. The record was not beaten — it was obliterated.

At 10:15 a.m. on the morning of Day Five, the Cedar River crested in Cedar Rapids at a whopping 31.12 feet, besting the old record by more than 11 feet and standing more than 19 feet above flood stage.

And fittingly, it was also Friday the 13th.

As word made its way downstream of the crush of water to the north, residents and city officials knew on Wednesday that a record crest would be there by Friday — but a record of 24.50 feet was projected, not the 31.12 feet it actually reached.

In part, the uncertainty was due to the loss of a key river gauge because of a power outage on Wednesday. The unit's back-up batteries failed, and the swift current of the river made it unsafe for officials to make their way by boat to fix the gauge.

On Thursday, water was already higher than the projected crest of 24.50 feet — by four feet. That reality led to a revised projection which was quite close to the actual Friday crest level.

Above: Flood water from the Cedar River nears the top of the street sign for 1st AVE NW and 1st Street NW in Cedar Rapids on the afternoon of Friday, June 13, 2008.

Opposite: The east channel around May's Island, Cedar Rapids, Iowa, on Friday, June 13, 2008.

JoAnn Wood

Jim Slosiarek/The Gazette

Jonathan D. Woods/The Gazette

Jim Slosiarek/The Gazette

Cliff Jette/The Gazette

Clockwise:

The Helen G. Nassif YMCA and Bills' Brothers Freight Salvage Furniture Liquidators and surrounding business were heavily damaged by flood water.

Sandbagging in the rain at Greene Square Park on Fourth Avenue SE in Cedar Rapids, Iowa on Thursday, June 12, 2008.

Volunteers form a human chain to carry sandbags for the effort of protecting Mercy Medical Center from the rising flood waters early Friday, June 13, 2008, in southeast Cedar Rapids.

Cedar Rapids city worker Dan Boyle and other city workers stack sandbags at Second St. SW and 16th Avenue SW on Thursday, June 12, 2008, in Cedar Rapids.

CV Radiographer Amber Holst (left), and Nurse Tracy Neurohr, continue to assist in sandbagging efforts as water creeps towards the front entrance of Mercy Medical Center in Cedar Rapids on Thursday, June 12, 2008.

Ashley O'Brien (right), 14, of Cedar Rapids hands a sandbag to Alex Novak (center), 15, of Walker and Tonya Cross (left, back to camera), 15, of Coggon as they and other volunteers form a human chain to carry sandbags for the effort of protecting Mercy Medical Center from the rising flood waters early Friday, June 13, 2008, in southeast Cedar Rapids.

Jim Slosiarek/The Gazette

6/13
Cedar River crested
on this date in 2008

12.00 ft.
Flood stage

20.00 ft.
Flood crest recorded
in 1851 & 1929

31.12 ft.
Flood crest on June 13, 2008

11.12 ft.
Higher flood crest than
either previous records
in 1851 or 1929

Cedar Rapids, Iowa

Photograph Liz Martin/The Gazette
National Weather Service Data

Clockwise: Water encroaches on the Cedar Rapids Police Department

Bruce Rentschler, far left, watches as a group of volunteers from J&J Custom Renovations loads his refrigerator onto a moving truck in preparation for the rising flood waters on Wednesday, June 11, 2008, in the Time Check neighborhood of Cedar Rapids.

Volunteers gather to fill sandbags on June 12, 2008.

The water rises on the evening of June 12, 2008 at Quaker Oats, Cedar Rapids, Iowa.

JoAnn Wood

Above: The Cedar Rapids Science Station on Thursday, June 12, 2008. At the crest, the flood water was several feet higher.

But some areas of Cedar Rapids had been under water for more than a week by that time, as the Cedar actually rose above flood stage back on June 2.

Many young people can recall their parents driving them across one of the three bridges that cross May's Island and connect west and east Cedar Rapids and hearing "the battleship story."

"You know, if you look down on May's Island from the air," the father might say, "it looks like a battleship floating in the river." The configuration of May's Island, with City Hall and the Linn County Courthouse on it, does indeed resemble a battleship when seen from that vantage point.

Hard for a young person to visualize from a ground-level view out a car window, though.

And sometimes hard to visualize when an aerial shot is taken, what with all the buildings on each side of the river and bridges sticking out from the island like tentacles.

It's far easier to spot a "battleship" when the bridges to the island are covered with water, and the island is truly out on its own in the middle of an ever-widening river.

And during the floods of 2008, the battle was certainly on.

The city was already tired of Mother Nature's games. Cedar Rapids had received double its normal snowfall during the previous winter. But mere snow was nothing compared with the uncontainable Cedar River.

MidAmerican Energy had cut natural gas service to 1,150 customers in threatened areas, including the Czech Village, as early as Tuesday night. The next morning, there were mandatory evacuations of the city within the 500-year flood plain — such as the Time Check, Osborn Park, and Cedar Valley/Rompot neighborhoods — as the river had already reached record levels.

The Linn County Jail was evacuated Thursday morning, and prisoners were transported by bus away from the quickly rising water. For some prisoners at the jail, the evacuation was déjà vu — some were actually moved there just the day before from Vinton, when the Benton County Jail was evacuated.

That evening, three downtown bridges were closed—those on First Avenue, Third Avenue, and Eighth Avenue, separating east from west at the heart of the downtown. They would remain closed for a full week before officials felt they were safe enough for travel. Traffic on Interstate 380 was also down to one lane in places. Pumps failed in southwest Cedar Rapids, and water began coming up through storm sewers on Wednesday.

On Wednesday afternoon, television station KCRG began continuous flood coverage. The ABC affiliate went wall-to-wall with flood news and information for several days, despite the fact that the station and its corporate sibling, *The Gazette*, were located in the evacuation zone. The newspaper and television station got special permission from the city to remain in

business, even as flood waters crept up to the corners of their building. The Iowa National Guard came to the station three separate times, urging KCRG to evacuate.

One of the signature buildings in Cedar Rapids, now known as the Alliant Energy Tower, was evacuated Thursday as water begin entering the first floor of the structure. Alliant's call center was also knocked out by the water, affecting customers throughout the Midwest. By Thursday afternoon, more than 15,000 Alliant customers were without power in Cedar Rapids, including the entire downtown area. KCRG stayed on the air through the use of generators, lowering light levels in the studio and turning off air conditioning to conserve power. Anchors even reported from stools on the street in front of their building, as viewers watched the flooding creep up the street toward them. With no running water in the building, the staff resorted to using portable toilets set up on the adjacent parking ramp. *The Gazette* powered a fully-computerized newsroom with on-site generators, and kept their *GazetteOnline* web site updated around the clock. On Thursday alone, the day before the crest, the paper's web site welcomed more than 111,000 unique users; the daily average is one-fifth of that amount.

But as they all quickly noted, whatever they were enduring was nothing compared with what citizens who lost homes and businesses would be facing.

KCRG anchors Bruce Aune and Beth Malicki were on the air for up to 12 hours a day themselves over a five day period surrounding the flooding. "There were more stories to cover than we could reach, more need than we could address, more destruction than we could fathom," Malicki later said.

KWWL's ability to cover the Cedar Rapids and Iowa City flooding was hampered by the water;

Liz Martin/The Gazette

John Armon

Top: A bus filled with inmates crosses the Third Avenue bridge as the Linn County Jail is evacuated due to rising floodwaters Thursday morning, June 12, 2008.

Bottom: Thursday, June 12th, 3rd Ave. SE looking west toward May's Island as a city bus evacuates prisoners from the Linn County Jail.

Opposite: Courthouse and jail on May's Island. Smoke rises from the basement of the jail where flood waters knocked out the generator. June 12, 2008.

their bureau on the first floor of the Alliant Tower quickly filled with water, and all the equipment there was destroyed.

North of the flooded area, other broadcast outlets were serving the public interest. WMT radio and KGAN-TV, both located in Broadcast Park, maintained non-stop coverage. KGAN even offered space in their building so two radio stations owned by Cumulus Media that had been flooded out of downtown facilities could get back on the air; a third Cumulus station took up residence in the conference room of KZIA radio — a direct competitor.

While radio station KMRY's studios on Blairs Ferry Road were dry, broadcasting was jeopardized because of the station's transmitter location, on Ellis Road NW. Massive efforts by the station's engineers and staff prevented all but a two-hour interruption in broadcasting. Engineers pulled two transmitters (the main signal generator and a back-up) from the soon-to-be-flooded transmitter site and climbed a 100-foot tower at the studio location to string a wire to feed the relocated transmitter — all during a driving rain storm on Thursday. That allowed KMRY to provide wall-to-wall coverage to listeners for the key days surrounding the crest of the river.

As did all broadcasters in the city, the station provided "essential information that just had to get out," according to KMRY owner Rick Sellers, regardless of the station's normal format. Commercials were suspended as necessary as the station broadcast live from a variety of sites around the city.

Tim Wilcox

KMRY was forced to use that patchwork system for a month, broadcasting with a limited signal, until the transmitter building was safe to reenter. Even then, the entire contents of the concrete building had to be replaced, down to the drywall and insulation.

The catastrophe of the 1993 flooding in Des Moines — losing a potable water supply — was a distinct possibility in Cedar Rapids when three of the city's four lateral water wells stopped working.

As the waters rose in Des Moines that year, the water treatment plant had become an island. Eventually, the river overtook the plant itself, and all water to the city was shut off. It took 12 days for the system to be restored for bathing and toilet flushing, and a full 19 days before the water was deemed safe for drinking.

The irony of fighting back record levels of one type of water, but having a loss of another type of water, was not lost on citizens who were lined up at distribution centers to get containers filled with safe water that had been hauled in by tanker truck.

Iowa's largest city went without tap water for nearly two weeks, and without drinking water for nearly three weeks. And now Iowa's second largest city was on the verge of a similar fate.

An estimated 1,200 volunteers sandbagged furiously late Thursday night to preserve the last functioning suction well. Power had been cut to both water treatment plants, and what little water the city had flowing — only a quarter of the normal amount — was in jeopardy as the Cedar continued to rise that final night before the crest.

Top: Looking north on 2nd Street SE over the sculpture entitled "Rapids" by David Black.

Bottom: Guy Ayers-Berry and his crew pilots his boat down 1st Avenue E en route to search for residents waiting to be evacuated in Cedar Rapids on Thursday evening, June 12, 2008.

Right: Third Avenue looking west, downtown Cedar Rapids, Iowa.

JoAnn Wood

Clockwise:

Downtown looking South toward the African American Historical Museum & Cultural Center of Iowa.

A flag remains on a flooded house on 2nd Avenue SW in Cedar Rapids on the afternoon of Friday, June 13, 2008.

First Street SW looking South toward the Penford plant.

The National Czech & Slovak Museum & Library in Cedar Rapids is several feet under water as the Cedar River continues to rise on Friday, June 13, 2008.

Liz Martin/The Gazette

Mike Schlotterback/Schlotterback Photographics

Cliff Jette/The Gazette

Greg Januska

Many saw the plea for volunteers on the 10 p.m. television news, and immediately, Edgewood Road was filled with those who wanted to make sure Cedar Rapids still had water. What had been a few people quickly grew to more than a thousand, and the job was swiftly done; the well was protected. Water use remained limited to drinking until the crisis passed.

Then as Thursday turned into Friday, the word went out that Mercy Medical Center was to be evacuated. Many of those who had worked to protect the last functioning well moved downtown to help at Mercy, located ten blocks from the Cedar River itself. The hospital had been without power since Thursday morning, but officials thought they would be safe from the onslaught of water and operated the facility with generated power.

By early evening, water began seeping into Mercy's basement, and officials decided to evacuate.

Volunteers were stacking sandbags around 1 a.m. Friday morning to keep the water out of the hospital's glass-walled Lundy Pavilion. The river water level was nearing 31 feet, with at least another foot predicted, and with a balky river gauge, there was really no telling just how bad it would get.

The volunteers would not be deterred, even as they stood in two feet of water and as lightning filled the sky. In the end, 50,000 sandbags were wrapped around Mercy that night. By 4 a.m., all "acute care" patients had been moved to other hospitals. Other patients were transported by bus to other facilities. The evacuation of 176 patients was completed around sunrise Friday morning, as two inches of water crept into the hospital's emergency room.

As the crest neared, 450 blocks of Cedar Rapids were under water, with some neighborhoods seeing standing water eight feet high. Longtime Linn County Sheriff Don Zeller was completing his last year in office before retirement when the crisis hit. "We're just kind of at God's mercy right now," he said at the time. "Hopefully, people that never prayed before this…it might be a good time to start."

As in Waterloo, another railroad bridge collapsed under the force of the water. This time, the debris from the collapsed bridge was made worse by the 20 hopper cars loaded with rocks that had been on the bridge. The cars were on the bridge to help weigh it down against the rising water.

But as a National Weather Service meteorologist noted, this was "uncharted territory," and as the bridge buckled, the mess from it and the rocks and the rail cars all made its way down the Cedar, causing more problems downstream.

Finally — finally — the high water mark came Friday morning. The Cedar had been out of its banks for 12 days, but the river levels finally began to fall.

Ultimately, 5,400 homes and 700 businesses were under water as a result of the Cedar's invasion into Cedar Rapids. About 1,300 city blocks were flooded. More than 20,000 residents, driven from their homes, were anxiously waiting to return to their neighborhoods after the crest to see what the Cedar had done to their lives. But even though waters had begun to fall, officials still needed to check areas for safety before allowing evacuees to return. More than once, officials told people they could return the next day, only to have that reentry delayed due to the immense amount of work the National Guard

Greg Januska

Above: A row of gondolas filled with gravel sit on the railroad bridge in Cedar Rapids. The cars were loaded onto the bridge in an attempt to keep the bridge attached to its moorings.

Opposite: The deluge of water proved to be too much, and the bridge collapsed on June 12 despite the efforts to fortify the railway.

Mike Schlotterback/Schlotterback Photographics

Top, Bottom: JoAnn Wood
Right: Theatre Cedar Rapids Below: Cliff Jette/The Gazette

Top: Flood water reaches almost as high as the awning on the Smulekoff's building.

Bottom: A chair from Smulekoff's was swept from the store and placed in a tree across the street.

Top Right: Theatre Cedar Rapids surrounded by flood waters.

"strike teams" had to do before reopening an area of the city, even temporarily. That led to tempers flaring at times; one reporter noted that "the outrage was overwhelming."

For evacuees, that was the worst part — not knowing what damage the river had caused, not knowing what was left of their homes, not knowing what they would do to fix whatever they found.

That sense of helplessness soon gave way to a new mixture of emotions. For some, it was relief that the Cedar's wrath was not as bad as they feared. For others, no words could properly convey what they found.

It was one thing to see furniture from Smulekoff's floating down what usually is First Street, after the river broke through store windows and carried couches out like a thief having a field day; it was another to open the door to one's home and see mud-coated belongings everywhere. From muck-sodden carpets, to now-stained family photos, the most personal and intimate parts of a person's life — their home, their safe place — had been invaded by the rudest of burglars.

Odd discussions followed, especially in the wake of the recent tornados in the area: Would you rather have your home struck by a tornado, or a flood? In a tornado, everything is gone and you have no hope of salvaging anything, but at least the cleanup is often limited; in a flood, you have to clean everything up and the items are often coated with foul water and residue, but you do have the possibility of finding treasured items.

It didn't matter. It was a flood, with everything that goes with it, including the cleanup.

With May's Island held captive by the river, local officials relocated quickly. By Monday, after the Friday morning crest, Cedar Rapids City Hall had moved to the AEGON building; other city and county offices set up shop in vacant space in the Westdale Mall facility; county court sessions were held at Kirkwood Community College.

When people saw how high the water had gotten at the downtown Paramount Theatre — up to the bottom of the lighted marquee over the entrance of the historic building — they knew it would be bad.

Bad didn't even begin to describe it.

The City of Cedar Rapids-owned facility was home to the Mighty Wurlitzer theatre pipe organ, installed when the building opened 80 years before and one of only 36 original installations remaining in the world. Nearly 800 instruments could be called into play on the organ, which originally cost $28,000.

In anticipation of the flood, members of the Cedar Rapids Area Theatre Organ Society — caretakers of the Wurlitzer and the Rhinestone Barton organ at the nearby Theatre Cedar Rapids location — raised the organ console at both locations to their highest levels. Cedar Rapids had claimed the distinction of being one of only three cities that had two working theatre organs in their original installations.

And then the waters came.

Thursday morning, the sandbags protecting the Paramount, which had most recently been restored just five years before, were breached. Water poured in all doors, well over the stage level. The key parts of the historic Wurlitzer were all waterlogged, and it would be nearly a week before anyone would know just how extensive the damage would be.

Janet Powell

Above: "The Village People" of hats were all lying in disarray after the waters receded from Theatre Cedar Rapids.

Opposite: Coonrod Wrecker and Crane Service employee John Mathis guides the Wurlitzer concert organ as a truck is used to pull it out of the flooded Paramount Theatre in downtown Cedar Rapids on Wednesday, June 18, 2008.

The Cedar River and Iowa River Valleys

The Cedar River has its headwaters in southern Minnesota, in Dodge County, just north of Austin, Minnesota. There is a west fork, a middle fork and an east fork. The three forks converge in Mower County and the Cedar flows into Iowa in Mitchell County. The endpoint is in Louisa County in southeast Iowa, where northeast of Columbus Junction, it joins the Iowa River and the Iowa flows on into the Mississippi River just north of Oakville. The Cedar River is also known as the Red Cedar River. It is named for cedar (juniper) trees that line its banks. The total length is approximately 300 miles.

The Iowa River is also approximately 300 miles in length. Its headwaters are in Hancock County, Iowa. There is a west and east fork that converge just north of Belmond in Wright County. It is one of the most scenic rivers in Iowa. South of Iowa Falls, the Iowa winds through a deeply carved scenic valley with high limestone cliffs. Just north of Iowa City, in Johnson and Iowa County, the Iowa is impounded to create the Coralville Reservoir. South of Iowa City, it is joined by the English River and north of Columbus Junction it is joined by the Cedar River. The Iowa flows into the Mississippi River just north of Oakville.

SOUTH DAKOTA

NEBRASKA

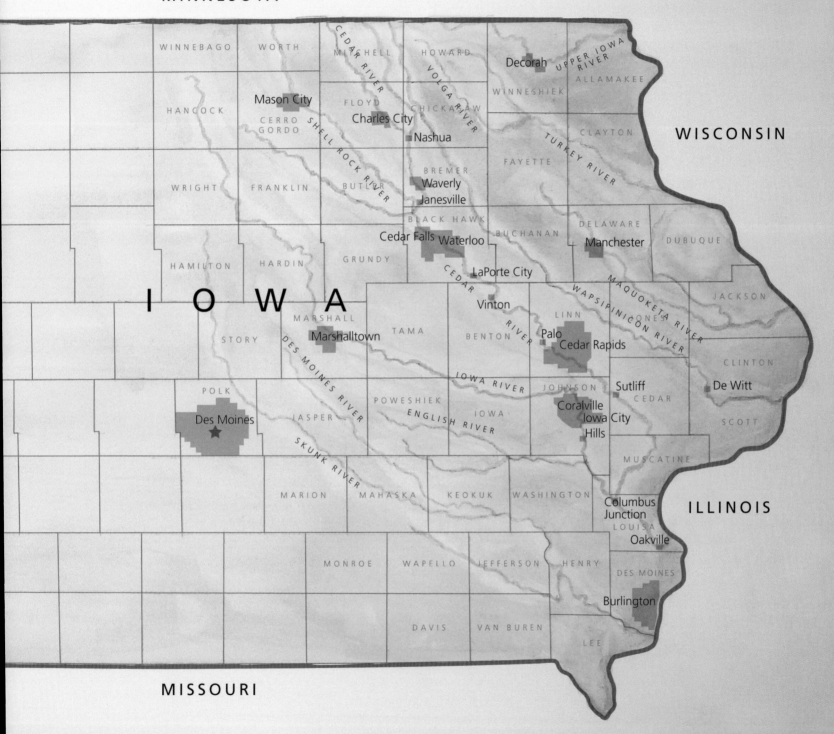

Top: The force of the flood water pushed in the lobby doors of the Paramount Theatre

The organ console was pushed off its lift by the force of waters reaching nine feet above the Paramount's stage. It was removed to assess what parts could be salvaged, finally breaking apart when it faced the outside sun for the first time since its installation in 1928.

About a month after the Wurlitzer was removed, the Rhinestone Barton was taken from Theatre Cedar Rapids and also moved to The History Center, where it stood face-to-face with the Wurlitzer, both unique pipe organs which had lived as neighbors in downtown Cedar Rapids for 80 years, awaiting repair, restoration, and hopefully, reinstallation.

In February 2009, the City Council voted to restore the Paramount, including the Mighty Wurlitzer, as part of a master plan for city buildings damaged by the flood, including the main Public Library, Police Station, Central Fire Station, and the Ground Transportation Center.

The Cedar Rapids animal control building took on seven feet of water during the flood. The city animal control center — to handle not only the animals who were then at the shelter, but the hundreds of pets who were left when homeowners in other parts of the city were evacuated — was temporarily moved to Kirkwood Community College, home of an agricultural sciences

John Armon

Left: 'H.W.' marks the high water mark near Mercy Medical Center, Cedar Rapids, Iowa, on Sunday, June 15, 2008.

Above: Lundy Pavillion/8th Ave. entrance of Mercy Medical Center after the facility was evacuated in the pre-dawn hours of Friday, June 13, 2008.

Mike Schlotterback/Schlotterback Photographics

program. Pet food donations from around the country arrived, and volunteers offered their services to keep the makeshift shelter operational. Ultimately, Kirkwood's Animal Health Technology Center was home to 1,000 animals — dogs, cats, and even ferrets.

A year later, the city's Animal Control department still operated from the college. There was no city animal shelter, but fundraising to establish a new shelter was underway.

Especially hard hit was the city's noted Czech Village, home to 30 businesses and the National Czech & Slovak Museum & Library. Debris deposited by the river, some of it large, was left behind when the water finally receded.

While business owners immediately expressed desire to rebuild, construction rules required the lowest level of most property there to be raised one foot above the flood plain level, which could jeopardize the rebirth of the area due to the high cost.

The museum, which opened in 1995, was inundated with ten feet of water in the flood. Repairing the museum's main building alone was estimated at $4 million, while a new exhibition center and research library to replace the original area could cost nearly $18 million more.

While important to the heritage of many, the facility also had positive impact on the city; the museum's 35,000 annual visitors provided $1 million annually in economic impact to Iowa.

Two semi-truck loads of artifacts had been moved to higher ground before the flood, while other items were moved to attics and upper levels of the museum and its collections facility. National and local experts came to the scene to ensure that cleanup of items after the waters receded proceeded appropriately. Textiles and flood–soaked linens came clean following careful

attention. Wash tubs, drying racks and clotheslines were lined up in the parking lot to facilitate cleaning of artifacts.

The great majority of books and papers were also saved. Staff members from the University of Iowa Libraries, led by preservation department head Nancy Kraft, came to help restore documents and artifacts, charging only enough to cover their costs. Kraft brought consultants in from around the country to help train UI staff members, who also helped in recovery efforts at the African American Historical Museum and Cultural Center of Iowa, located in Cedar Rapids. The UI also offered to store damaged items, rent-free, for as long as necessary.

That could be a long time.

The museum reopened in a new, temporary location with an inaugural exhibit on the flood itself and its impact on the Czech Village. Officials are focusing on taking a series of traveling exhibits around the country to keep the facility vibrant and front-of-mind while decisions are made about rebuilding and the future.

As for the Village itself, businesses are slowly reopening as they can. But a large number of homes in the neighborhood will not be rebuilt. The neighborhood as citizens knew it, like so many others, will never be the same.

For many downtown businesses, whose street-level storefronts had been crushed by the water, there was little to do but clear the area and start over, once it was safe. But even those who had offices in higher, drier stories of downtown buildings were affected, since they could not get into their offices for days due to safety concerns.

Janet Powell

Above: The interior of The National Czech & Slovak Museum & Library in Cedar Rapids, Iowa.

Opposite: The Czech Village area of Cedar Rapids, Iowa was one of the hardest hit areas. Clockwise: Sykora Bakery, a worker mans sump pumps outside a village business, and Polehna's Meat Market.

John Armon

Courtney Sargent/The Gazette

Above: Homes show the marks of dirt and grime. Flood water completely submerged these homes.

Above right: Karen Teel (right) hugs Bonnie Dean of the Humane Society of Missouri thanking her for saving her pets that were trapped in her apartment on First Street and Sixth Avenue in Cedar Rapids on Saturday, June 14, 2008. Eleven cats, 18 rats and 2 birds were removed from the apartment and taken to Kirkwood Community College to be housed.

The Cedar Rapids Area Chamber of Commerce coordinated an effort to let people back into their offices for a limited time, and under strict supervision, to retrieve important items because their buildings would not be deemed safe for regular occupancy for some time — and it would be even longer before "business as usual" was a phrase that could be used. Chamber officials escorted "essential downtown business owners" to their offices only a day after the river crest.

"We couldn't believe that this was the city we knew," according to Amy Johnson Boyle, who was then marketing and communications director for the Chamber, and who led one of the first groups across the skywalk system. Roughly 1,000 people were waiting to be among those who could retrieve the items they needed to carry on their businesses, and their lives.

Looking through the skywalk and seeing the river raging through downtown, carrying cars, dumpsters and debris, was the "scariest, eeriest feeling I've ever felt," she said. Armed with a flashlight and a bull horn, she and others entered from the parkade near the U.S. Cellular Center, not knowing quite what they would find.

Only those with apartments or businesses on the second floor or higher were allowed in; officials feared it was not safe to let people go down to the lower levels due to the water, toxins, sewage — and even the possibility of bodies of those who did not evacuate in time and were caught by the rising river. There was also concern that the skywalks themselves might not be

Liz Martin/The Gazette

Liz Martin/The Gazette

structurally safe. Some officials were more than a little hesitant to allow anyone back in the buildings — at any level — so soon after the crest.

Heavy rains from above leaking in, and humidity from the water below, turned the skywalk trip into a treacherous nightmare. Trash, ceiling tiles, buckled carpet and darkness of buildings without power made a trip across the city on the skywalk take 45 minutes; it normally took only 10.

Business owners and residents retrieved whatever they could carry, from computers, files and records to plants and even animals. Despite the high humidity, hot temperatures, and smelly conditions, the groups remained "remarkably orderly — but scared," Boyle noted.

Then on the way back, her group detected the smell

of gas. Firefighters shut down the remaining planned retrievals for the day, until the matter was resolved. Indeed, there was a gas leak in one of the buildings, caused by the flood, demonstrating the continued need for caution even though the worst of the flooding was over.

In the end, the skywalk retrievals continued on Sunday, after the gas leak was repaired. Despite it all, there were no injuries, incidents, or major arguments, even though "your world as you knew it was completely gone, turned upside down," she said.

The skywalk system itself would not reopen to the public until mid-November.

On Saturday, June 21, eight days after the high water mark, the Cedar River level dropped below flood stage in Cedar Rapids for the first time since June 2.

Above Left: President George W. Bush is greeted by former Iowa governor Bob Ray, center, and former Iowa first lady Billie Ray after landing at the Eastern Iowa Airport to visit flooded areas on Thursday, June 19, 2008. U.S. Senator Tom Harkin (D-Iowa) is at right.

Above Right: Marine One flies over flooded areas of Coralville as President George W. Bush surveys damage from recent flooding in the Cedar Rapids and Iowa City areas on Thursday, June 19, 2008.

Above: A makeshift sign reading "Good by Time Check" (sic) rests along the sidewalk in the Time Check neighborhood in Northwest Cedar Rapids on Friday, June 27, 2008. Forty homes in Cedar Rapids have been scheduled for demolition; 18 of those homes are in the northwest quadrant.

Above Right:
A devastated home on O Ave. NW in the Time Check neighborhood is marked with caution tape.

Opposite:
(Clockwise) Belongings damaged in last year's flood line a Time Check neighborhood street in Northwest Cedar Rapids on Friday, June 20, 2008.

Theatre Cedar Rapids makes a statement on its marquee. Messages like this one were written all around damagaed neighborhoods.

Two "American Gothic"-style mannequins remained standing outside the Cedar Rapids Freedom Festival Office after the flood waters receded. The 2008 Freedom Festival had to be postponed and celebrated during Labor Day weekend due to flooding.

Urban Search and Rescue team member and Cedar Rapids firefighter Eric Vandewater of North Liberty marks the Czech Village Salvation Army as unsafe to enter on Monday, June 16, 2008, in Southwest Cedar Rapids.

And even more devastation was revealed.

Some displaced residents received an early Independence Day gift, as the first FEMA mobile homes arrived in Cedar Rapids for use as temporary housing on Wednesday, July 2. But that feeling of independence was short-lived for some. After receiving complaints about trailer residents becoming ill, television station KGAN did a special report testing the homes, and found potentially unsafe levels of formaldehyde in several of the homes. That report prompted Gov. Chet Culver to write the head of FEMA to express his concern.

Later, Barnes & Noble Booksellers in Cedar Rapids conducted its annual Memoir Writing Contest for Fourth and Fifth Grade Students. The theme was, "How I Will Remember 2008." Entries ranged from vacation experiences, to memorable moments in sports, to challenges and triumphs at school. The

winner, Alex Fernandez, a fifth grader at Cleveland Elementary School, wrote an essay that brought tears to the eyes of those attending the reception to honor the writers. That essay about the record flood, exactly as it was written by the 10-year-old, is as follows:

My name is Alex Fernandez. I am 10½ years old. I am from Cedar Rapids, Iowa. I chose to write about the Flood of 2008. Seven months ago, there was a terrible and destructive flood that hit most of Iowa, including Cedar Rapids. I kept a journal and wrote everything that had happened in that terrifying summer of 2008. I have shared some of my feelings in the journal. The flood was very devastating for the people of Cedar Rapids. The force of the water just ruined people's homes and lives. People watched as there homes were destroyed. Then about 2-3 days after the flood it crested. About a week later the water was back in the river but the destruction

Liz Martin/The Gazette

Theatre Cedar Rapids

Liz Martin/The Gazette

Mike Schlotterback/Schlotterback Photographics

was everywhere. My grandparents were evacuated Wednesday, June 11, and didn't get back into their home until June 20.

On June 13th, my mom got to go an a boat to rescue our cat, Cosmo. He was older so we thought he would be ok there. The Army National Guards told us that it might be weeks before my grandparents got back into their house. So she got in the boat and they took her to my grandmas. She said the water was up to the roof of the porch. She also said it was scary to be inside the house full of water. The man found Cosmo under a bed upstairs and they all got back in the boat and came back to the checkpoint.

You cannot believe the way the house looked when I finally got to see it for the first time. I didn't even know what to say. We were all speechless. I was shocked. My little sister cried. My grandma, my mom and aunts cried. It looked like there had been a war. It smelled really bad and everybody was wearing masks.

Furniture was thrown everywhere and the living room TV was thrown forward had shattered. The refrigerator was tipped sideways. Our family knew that to rebuild it would take a lot of work. I looked around and saw many of my things covered in black mud. They said it was too hard to save anything. My skateboard, fishing pole, movies, clothes, and my pictures were all piled in front of the house by the street, along with the rest of the memories of my grandparent's house. I was very sad.

Army trucks drove up and down the street. People were walking around everywhere talking to neighbors. They were all sad. They hugged and cried. People that did not live by my grandma's house would drive by the houses and point and shake their heads or take pictures. I guess they wanted to remember. I will never forget.

Now the house was empty. You could see the mark from the flood water on the walls. It was almost to the ceiling. I tried to imagine what it was like. My grandpa and uncles have been working really hard on the house everyday. They ripped all the walls out. I got to help. Everybody worked hard and even my brother and I helped knock out walls. Even though the flood didn't go upstairs my grandpa said the mold could have went up there too. Now they have a new house inside. It has painted walls, new floors, new basement. They are starting to run out of money so my grandma is talking to a lot of people in the city to help flood victims.

Nearly a year later, Grandma and Grandpa's house is not finished. Close, but not yet. I cannot wait to get back to their house. My brother, sister and I have rooms there for when we spend the night. It is our other home. There will also be floods, hurricanes, tornadoes and other natural disasters. I only hope that I will never see another one in my lifetime like the flood I saw when I was ten.

Alex is not the only one.

Linn County Engineering and Secondary Road Department

Above: The driveway on the river side of the Linn County Courthouse on May's Island was washed away by flood water.

Opposite

(Left) Large pumps pull water from the building that is the home of the Cedar Rapids Freedom Festival office on Second Street SE.

(Top Right) The Veterans Memorial Window by Grant Wood at Cedar Rapids' City Hall remains intact on Tuesday, June 17, 2008, after floodwaters receded from the building. Puddles and mud cover the floor of the building, which took on about a foot and a half of water on the first floor.

(Bottom Right) The historic Vavra home at 1019 3rd St SE, future site of the Oak Hill Jackson community garden.

Mike Schlotterback/Schlotterback Photographics

Doug Lambert

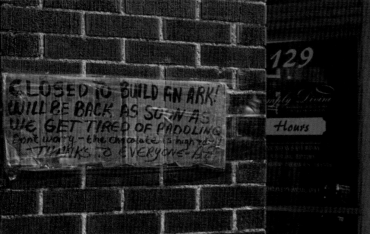

Louis Collins

Mike Schlotterback/Schlotterback Photographics

Mike Schlotterback/Schlotterback Photographics

DO YOU LIVE HERE ARE YOU HERE TO HELP IF NOT! GET OUT

RIVER OF TEARS

HUGE BLOCK PARTY 6-12-08

The Iowa National Guard

Saturday, June 14, 2008

Tale of Two Cities

Jonathan D. Woods/The Gazette

The sound was achingly familiar by now.

First, the creaking of ancient wood. Then, the snapping of metal support braces. Finally, a surprisingly quiet sound as a piece of history disappeared from the horizon.

This time, it was the Sutliff Bridge, built in 1896. The bridge, made up of three arching steel spans with wooden planks, was on the National Register of Historic Places. It was one of the last and longest wooden bridges of its kind in Iowa, located about 25 miles north of Iowa City. As a fundraiser, people had even purchased planks of the bridge, so personal was the connection between visitors and the triple-arch structure.

Shortly after noon on Friday, the eastern third collapsed under the force of the rushing Cedar River, and with it, another century of memories.

Those in Charles City knew what that was like; they lost their iconic bridge on Day One. Railroad bridges collapsed in Waterloo and Cedar Rapids, too, but those losses weren't the same.

The day after the Sutliff Bridge succumbed, Day Six, the few sightseers who could make their way to the bridge saw a hole in the sky that could never be filled. But with so many roads closed by the overflow of the Cedar and Iowa Rivers in the area, sightseers were indeed few.

After more than 25 years of concentrated growth, the gap was closing between Iowa City and Cedar Rapids. It used to be easy to tell where one ended and the other began, because very little business or development was seen along that 20-mile span of Interstate 380. In recent years, economic development proponents promoted a "corridor" between the two major Iowa cities, and getting from one to the other seemed quicker despite the fact that the geographic distance was the same.

The I-380 corridor was closed at 6 p.m. on Friday, splitting the two cities just as rivers up and down the line had split individual towns into separate islands. Those who commuted from one of the towns along I-380 to either major city could not get to work as usual for days, and I-380 between the cities did not open until the next Tuesday.

That didn't really matter. Given the destruction on both sides, it was hardly business as usual, anyway.

Above: Iowa National Guard Staff Sgt. Tonya Wegner smiles as she is covered in mud during a sandbagging operation at Baculis Mobile Home Park in Iowa City on Monday, June 16, 2008. The crew worked for hours to boost the integrity of the levee keeping the park from flooding out.

Opposite: U.S. Soldiers assigned to the Iowa Army National Guard construct a 7-foot levee to protect an electrical generator from rising floodwaters in Hills, Iowa, on Saturday, June 14, 2008.

Art Self/The Daily Iowan

Lindsey Walters/The Daily Iowan

Jonathan D. Woods/The Gazette

Brian Ray/The Gazette

(Top Left and Right) Campus flood preparations on Friday, June 13, 2008 primarily around the Main Library and the Lindquist Center.

Iowa Memorial Union on The University of Iowa campus Wednesday, June 11, 2008 in Iowa City. The water from the river was expected to reach close to the top of the wall being built.

Volunteers sandbag business and homes in the Iowa River Landing area of Coralville, Iowa Friday, June 13, 2008 as floodwaters rise in the area after a sandbag dike broke at the corner of Edgewater Drive and Quarry Road.

Iowa Medical Classification Center inmates Eusebio Limas (left) and John Dehner (right) work with Army Reserve PFC Tiffany Reed of Coralville (center) to increase the height of a sandbag wall behind the Days Inn Hotel Wednesday, June 11, 2008 in Coralville, Iowa.

Sandbagging efforts continue as floodwaters continue to rise along the Iowa River on Normandy Dr. in Iowa City, Iowa on Monday, June 9, 2008.

Volunteers help fill and fasten sandbags at The University of Iowa Main Library on Friday, June 13, 2008.

Ralph Sauer, left, and Mark Poggenpohl, center, toss sandbags onto a tractor scoop. The sandbags will be taken around the property at Thatcher & Baculis Mobile Home Park to build onto a wall keeping flooding back.

Brian Ray/The Gazette

Brian Ray/The Gazette

Above: The future of the 110-year-old Sutliff Bridge over the CedarRiver remains uncertain after a span was washed out during the June 2008 floods.

Opposite: The Iowa River at the intersection of Highway 27/218 and Highway 22. The Riverside Casino and Golf Resort are right center.

Most attention had focused on the Cedar's massive flow. But the Iowa River had been setting records of its own. From Marshalltown to Marengo, the Iowa gained momentum as it angled toward Coralville, and then Iowa City.

The crest came on Sunday, June 15, but it was a slow, tortuous process.

The Coralville Dam is designed to protect against flooding caused by the Iowa River. The river's outflow is managed to keep the river level south of the dam stable.

But there was no managing the force of the flood of 2008, here or anywhere else.

There was plenty of warning, however, and plenty of attempts to ward off the worst. Sandbagging in the area actually began 11 days before the river finally crested. The same day sandbagging began, June 4, the

University of Iowa evacuated the Mayflower Residence Hall, located across Dubuque Street from the river to the east. The next day, that low-lying street was closed and neighborhoods in both Coralville and Iowa City began taking on flood water.

That was days before Mason City in northern Iowa was under water, and before this One Week in June even began.

On Sunday, June 8, one full week before the high water crest of this flood, the Iowa River exceeded the 22-foot flood stage. It would not drop below flood stage for a full month.

Lower areas often flood, folks thought. How bad could this get? Could it really get as bad as 1993, when a then-record water level seven feet above flood stage was reached?

Vivian and Marc Saegesser

Above: Lightning flashes in the sky as a storm front moves over the Coralville Lake emergency spill way at 2 a.m. on Tuesday, June 10, 2008.

Brian Ray/The Gazette

Brian Ray/The Gazette

It could. And worse.

Water first began to trickle over the spillway at the Coralville Dam at 5 p.m. on Tuesday, just as the Cedar was cresting in Janesville; by 9 p.m. that evening, as 4,000 volunteers were furiously sandbagging to save downtown Cedar Falls, the trickle had become a flow.

And that was just the beginning. Officials knew that once water went over the Dam, they could not control the flow and what happened next was up to nature. It was just the second time in its 50-year history that water went over the spillway.

In the early morning hours of Thursday, the Normandy Drive/Parkview Terrace neighborhood in Iowa City was evacuated; citizens were awakened and taken away in the middle of the night.

And with good reason. Around 10 a.m., eight hours after the evacuation, the levee near that neighborhood failed. Later on Thursday, Iowa City's Idyllwild neighborhood and Gilbert Street business area, and Coralville's Edgewater Drive neighborhood, were all evacuated.

Meanwhile, a few miles away, an embankment holding tracks for the CRANDIC (Cedar Rapids and Iowa City) railway began to erode due to the Iowa River's force on the other side and the surging Clear Creek. Once holes developed on Thursday, water began

Above Left: Iowa City Police Investigator Mike Smithey (right) and Officer Abe Schabilion knock on the door of a home on Normandy Drive in Iowa City at 1:45 a.m. on Thursday, June 12, 2008 after a mandatory evacuation order was issued.

Above: Iowa City Police Officer Matt Huber carries Luke Thompson, 4, as he helps evacuate the family from their home on Eastmoore Drive on Thursday, June 12, 2008.

6/15
Iowa River crested
on this date in 2008

22.00 ft.
Flood stage

28.52 ft.
Flood crest recorded in 1993

31.53 ft.
Flood crest on June 15, 2008

3.02 ft.
Higher flood crest than
previous record in 1993

Iowa City, Iowa

Photograph: Lindsey Walters/The Daily Iowan
National Weather Service Data

Right: Flood waters from the swollen Iowa River threaten a sandbag wall near Iowa Memorial Union in Iowa City on Saturday afternoon, June 14, 2008.

Above: Signs on the main doors of the Iowa Memorial Union announce the closure of the facility Friday, June 13, 2008 in Iowa City. Floodwaters from the Iowa River were nearing the top of the sandbag levee protecting the building.

Opposite: Houses off of Foster Road sit in the floodwaters on Tuesday, June 10, 2008. A sandbag wall protects the homes of others.

filling the Coralville business strip and covering U.S. Highway 6 connecting Coralville to Iowa City. At its peak, the strip was filled with five feet of standing Iowa River water, turning a once-thriving section of restaurants and other businesses into block after block of river-soaked devastation.

The area had flooded during the previous record in 1993…but not like this. Nothing had ever been like this.

Local radio station KCJJ's studios are located in the Iowa River Landing in Coralville. On Friday morning, just as the crest was near in Cedar Rapids, station owner and morning co-host Steve Soboroff was at work, preparing to go on the air. At 4:20 a.m., the station signal went dead. The digital telephone line the station uses to send its signal from the studio to the off-site transmitter — which was controlled through Qwest facilities in Cedar Rapids — was lost due to the flooding to the north.

The easy thing would have been to simply close up shop and let nature win. Instead, "Captain Steve" and morning co-host Tommy Lang grabbed what equipment they could — CDs, news copy, headphones, and the machine that played commercials — and set up shop at the station's transmitter site, directly feeding a signal over the air through an auxiliary control board kept at the transmitter for emergencies — like this.

KCJJ's morning program, "The Big Show," was on the air by 5:30 a.m., and the format for programming changed immediately; the station went wall-to-wall with flood information for five straight days, and then stayed with flood-related programming (except for overnight hours) for another five days — all from the transmitter site.

They would have had to broadcast from there anyway, because not long after they left, water reached the studios of "The Mighty 1630" itself, though not at

Above: Iowa City Firefighters Tina McDermott and Darrall Brick use a rubber boat to evacuate Paul Measells of Normandy Drive in Iowa City after the truck he was being evacuated in stalled in floodwaters Thursday, June 12, 2008. Measells was unable to walk out of the area because of a medical condition.

Opposite: Onlookers watch floodwater flow from underneath the Burlington Street bridge on Saturday, June 14, 2008.

Top Right: Tiffin Volunteer Firefighters Jack Eggers (left) and Ray Forman (right) help Coralville resident Karen Spieker out of a boat and to her wheel chair Friday, June 13, 2008 as flood waters from Clear Creek cover Highway 6 in Coralville. Spieker and her husband Frank had to be evacuated from their apartment after the floodwaters prevented their son from coming to get them.

Bottom Right: Water flows under the sand bags and into the parking lot of the IMU on Friday, June 13, 2008.

Lindsey Walters/The Daily Iowan

Jonathon D. Woods/The Gazette

Above: Bill Garner and Dave Anderson paddle back to the AT&T building on Highway 6 in Coralville as floodwaters from Clear Creek and the Iowa River rise in Coralville on Friday afternoon, June 13, 2008.

Opposite: The Coralville Strip sits among the Iowa River floodwaters on Monday, June 16, 2008.

the levels seen on the Coralville strip. Sales and business departments operated out of staff members' homes for nearly two weeks.

Using a system improvised out of necessity — a microphone pointed at a speaker phone the duo bought at a local superstore in those pre-dawn hours — KCJJ aired calls from city officials, emergency workers, and regular listeners to keep the community informed during a time of tremendous need.

As the horrors of what had happened to downtown Cedar Rapids became known, and with water continuing to drown businesses in Coralville, on Friday the University of Iowa abandoned non-essential operations and suspended classes, as well as evacuated flood-prone buildings. Focus was placed on protecting the southern part of campus, that part integrated with the city's downtown. There was already damage to the campus, but 15 years of progress and building since the 1993 flood put even more university property at risk, especially if the water was going to top the old record, which it quickly did.

The 1993 Iowa River record in Iowa City of 28.52 was surpassed on Friday. And the water kept coming.

Protecting the campus became more difficult when the projections for river levels changed; in some places, dike systems were built three times to keep up with the expected crest, since there is a limit to how high a sandbag wall can be built in order to be effective. For example, at the UI, a two-foot-tall, six-foot-wide sandbag wall built one day would need to be replaced with a higher and stronger "Jersey barrier" made of precast concrete the next day if the river forecast increased; that, in turn, was replaced in

some areas by a "HESCO barrier," a series of collapsible mesh containers with fabric lining that can hold sand, dirt or gravel.

The university's Museum of Art carefully packed 80 percent of its collection — some 10,000 pieces of art — and shipped it away to safety; the rest was moved to higher ground locally.

As water continued to rise, projections indicated that the crest would come on Monday at 33 feet, more than four feet above the 1993 record. Water was already lapping at the bottom of downtown bridges, and at 33 feet, the water would have covered them, as happened in Cedar Rapids.

The focus of protection had moved to the southern part of campus before the weekend; there was nothing else that could be done for the arts campus area. Faculty and staff were told then that some campus buildings might be closed until at least August, and that they might want to pack and clear their offices accordingly.

The main UI electrical power plant was shut down in the early hours of Saturday morning, after sections of the riverside facility began to take on water. More than 2,000 volunteers worked on Day Six on campus, presenting a unified "last push" against the potential flood crest despite thunderstorms and heavy rain that forced brief interruptions in the effort.

Meanwhile, other volunteers helped move books to higher levels of the UI Main Library, fearing the worst of the river projections. Faculty, staff and students helped relocate video production equipment, including a full television studio, from the first floor of the journalism building to higher ground.

Brian Ray/The Gazette

Nick (Tha_Nsr)

Above: The Coralville Dam and spillway send floodwaters down river on Monday, June 16, 2008. The reservoir crested at 717 feet on Sunday night, June 15.

In order to keep communication lines open, the UI moved its normal web site address to an off-campus "Blogspot" account, in the event the university's computing center lost power or took on water. The "Blogspot" address became popular for weeks after the flood as a place where students, faculty, staff, alumni and members of the public could go for information, and was updated as flood-related matters warranted through the first quarter of 2009.

A nighttime curfew was imposed Saturday night in Iowa City and Coralville for floodwater areas, including the campus itself.

But then, a break — the water not only crested earlier, but lower than expected, partly because so much rushed into Coralville due to the CRANDIC breach.

Around 6:30 a.m. Sunday, the high water mark was reached in Iowa City at 31.53 feet, three feet more than the record. Four feet of water blocked one entrance to the Iowa Memorial Union, and the nearby Danforth Chapel had taken on water, as well. But other than water in basements, the new Adler Journalism and Mass Communication Building, Becker Communication Studies Building and Main Library were dry, and at the nearby Lindquist Center, home to the university's computer system, the only water that touched the sandbag walls there came from a light rain that fell Saturday.

In fact, once the crest was confirmed, sandbag volunteers continued to show up — this time, to fill remaining bags with sand already on site and to

Julie Koehn/The Daily Iowan

remove unneeded bags to be sent further down river, to help those who would be affected next.

Staff members at *The Daily Iowan* student newspaper were forced to evacuate their home in the journalism building, which had four feet of water in its basement. But they still covered the biggest story of their young careers, publishing a six-page edition on Monday using facilities elsewhere on campus and office space donated by *The Gazette.*

More than 600 Iowa City homes were evacuated during the flood; another 500 families were displaced in Coralville.

Ultimately, 23 buildings at the University of Iowa were closed for a time, with the most lasting

devastation hitting the Arts Campus; the inside of the noted Hancher Auditorium was completely destroyed, with water reaching the stage where so many historic performances had taken place, and the Voxman Music Building was filled up to the first floor, leading to the loss of two dozen pianos left behind as the water quickly rose. The total cost to repair the university was estimated at $231.75 million.

Work would begin quickly, and there were some early victories. The Mayflower Residence Hall, which originally was presumed to be closed for a year, actually opened in time for the 2008-2009 academicyear. After a brief interruption, summer school resumed at the

Above: The UI Theatre Building still sits in several inches of water on Thursday, June 19, 2008. Sandbag efforts to line the sidewalk near the Iowa Arts Buildings did not hold back the river.

Jonathan D. Woods/The Gazette

Brian Ray/The Gazette

Jonathan D. Woods/The Gazette

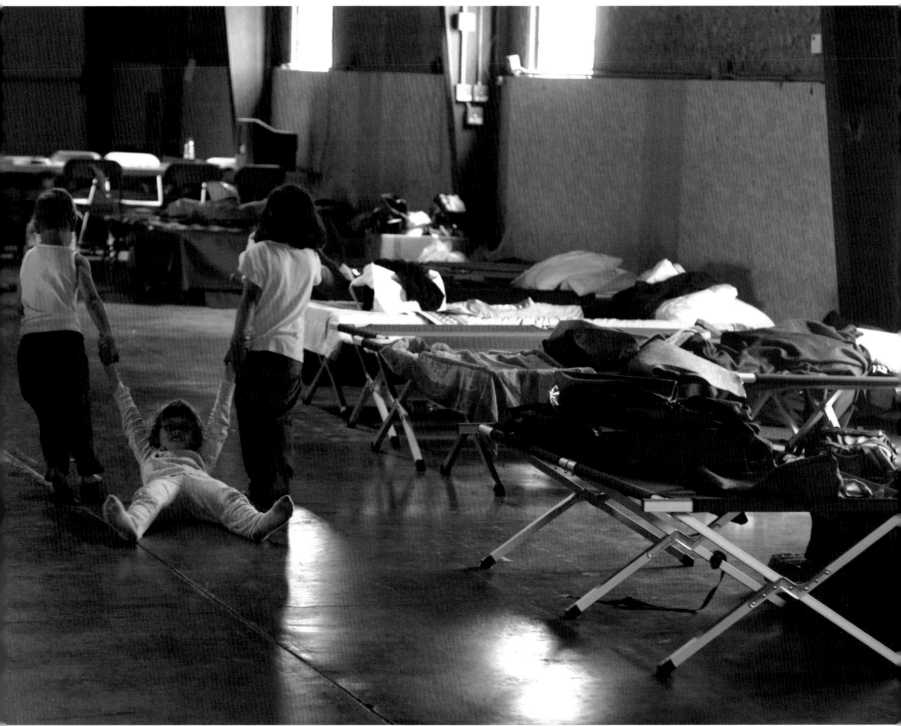

Jonathan D. Woods/The Gazette

UI a week after the river crested, with a record number of students, and fall classes went on as scheduled — although often in different places — by August.

A year later, there is still discussion about what to do to restore the university's arts campus facilities, and how to retain the charm of being nestled along the banks of the Iowa, while at the same time avoiding losses like those that occurred in 2008.

After all that had happened in a furious week, things settled back down on campus; however, homes that had never had flooding before were devastated, partly because of the record-high water, and partly because of new building in the region that changed the diffusion of the water from past flood events. Businesses on the Coralville strip struggled to take stock of their livelihoods, and decide whether it was worth it to reopen.

And almost unnoticed, weeks later, a milestone. On Monday, July 7, the river level dropped below flood stage in Iowa City for the first time since June 8 — a full month of flooding.

Above: Flood waters from the Iowa River surround Old Chicago Pizza on Hwy. 6 in Coralville on Monday, June 16, 2008.

Opposite:
Cheyen Blackburn, 8, plays with friends by the cots where they sleep at the Johnson County Fairgrounds in Iowa City, Iowa on June 16, 2008.

Above: Volunteer Reggie Schulte removes items destroyed by flood waters from the basement of St. Wenceslaus Church on Thursday, June 19, 2008.

Right: Jaclyn Donmyer of Iowa City holds a sign directing people into Iowa City West High School's parking lot before Parkview Evangelical Free Church's morning service on Sunday, June 15, 2008.

Left: Water continues to rise on a sidewalk outside the IMU on Sunday, June 15, 2008. The Danforth Chapel was completely surrounded by flood water and debris despite sand-bagging efforts.

Opposite Right: Volunteer Bret Loes, a teacher from Washington D.C., takes a break from gutting the basement of St. Wenceslaus Church on Thursday, June 19, 2008. After seeing the effects of the flood, Loes felt compelled to help, so he drove to Iowa and started volunteering.

Phoebe Webb/The Daily Iowan

John Armon

Greg Freiden

Evil Sivan

Joseph L. Murphy/IFBF

Sunday, June 15, 2008
Come Hell or High Water

Opposite & Above: Volunteers work to build a levee near Columbus Junction, Iowa.

They worked day and night for five days, placing 100,000 sandbags to fortify existing levees and create new barriers on the east side of Columbus Junction. The 1,900 residents were facing a double whammy — their community is where the Cedar River and the Iowa River merge. The full force of both swollen rivers was headed their way, and city officials began preparations Tuesday, before the Cedar River had even crested in Waverly.

But by Sunday morning, the water had won. Yet the spirit of the citizens remained intact.

A mile-long sandbag levee was built along Iowa Highway 92, another was built along the eastern edge of the town, tying into the first, while a third was put in place along Iowa Highway 70.

Columbus Junction residents were quite used to flooding in 2008. Two of the top six all-time record floods had occurred earlier that spring, thanks to winter snow melt and early spring rains.

But nothing could stop 32.5 feet of river, a level that smashed the 1993 record by more than four feet.

An earthen levee gave way late Saturday afternoon. Then another. The water began washing out the rail bed, and the fight was over.

Water came rushing into the community, drowning not only the downtown but also the town's water plant. By Sunday morning, water was ten feet high in parts of the city, nearly to the roofs of two dozen businesses. By the time of the official crest Monday morning, the downtown had even more water in it.

The senior center. The medical center. The pharmacy. The lifeblood of any small Iowa town — all under a dozen feet of water from the Iowa River, thanks to breaches in three levees Saturday evening.

By Monday, Gov. Chet Culver visited. While waiting for Culver's arrival, Columbus Junction Mayor Dan Wilson spoke to 100 persons who had gathered in the high school gymnasium.

"We didn't get beat," he told them. "We may not have accomplished everything we wanted to, but don't go home thinking we lost."

The mayor said the community spirit of his town had been phenomenal, despite the devastating rush of water. People worked together. They bonded. They had a plan and executed it flawlessly. Culver called

6/16
Cedar and Iowa Rivers converged and crested on this date in 2008

19.00 ft.
Flood stage

28.30 ft.
Flood crest recorded in 1993

32.49 ft.
Flood crest on June 16, 2008

4.19 ft.
Higher flood crest than previous record in 1993

Columbus Junction,

Photograph Joseph L. Murphy/IFBF
National Weather Service Data

Iowa

Joseph L. Murphy/IFBF

Joseph L. Murphy/IFBF

The Columbus Gazette

The Columbus Gazette

Columbus Junction the best-prepared town he had seen.

But in a city located just south of the convergence of two swollen rivers, no amount of preparation could have been enough.

Early on Day Seven, the Cedar River crested in Conesville at 10.4 feet above flood stage, more than five feet above the record. Meanwhile, as the sun came up in Iowa City, the Iowa River crested there at nearly 10 feet above flood stage, besting the 15-year record by three feet.

Clearly, Columbus Junction did not stand a chance. But no one told the citizens that. And if someone had, they would have fought anyway. They lived through three historic floods in six weeks, refusing to quit sandbagging when "the big one" was near until physically forced to stop by city officials.

Saturday — the day the first levee failed — the Iowa National Guard 3655th Maintenance Repair Company reported for duty, assisting Columbus Junction residents with flood operations. Among them was 28-year-old Spc. Curtis White.

The call for duty came at an inopportune time for White – he was to be married four days later. Clearly, given the devastation caused by the flooding, the Guard would still be on duty then and the wedding would have to be postponed.

Postponed again, that is — the couple had already delayed their wedding day three times for various reasons.

That was when Danielle Ritter, White's fiancée, had enough. No more postponements, she said. The 29-year-old transplanted Georgian called city officials to ask about a civil wedding ceremony right there in Columbus Junction.

It turns out a wedding was just what this town needed.

A mere three days after the river had crested, a Guard chaplain performed the ceremony on a state highway bridge overlooking a breached levee. Mayor Wilson escorted the bride down a makeshift outdoor aisle.

She was wearing a T-shirt reading "Come Hell or High Water."

Republican presidential candidate John McCain, in town to tour the city's damage, presented the couple with a wedding gift and wished them a happy and long marriage.

It certainly started memorably — for them, and for a community that needed a reminder of hope and renewal amid record devastation.

Less than a week later, however, there was even more damage, as a railroad bridge over the Iowa River collapsed near Columbus Junction, sending a locomotive, two railcars and the engineer into the water late one evening. The cars were on the bridge originally to provide weight to protect the structure from washing away during the high point of the flood.

Ironically, the structure failed as rail employees were pulling the tanker cars off the bridge.

The Columbus Gazette

Above: Iowa National Guard Spc. Curtis White married Danielle Ritter in a civil ceremony by a Guard chaplain in Columbus Junction, Iowa.

Opposite:
(Top left and top right) Iowa National Guard servicemen work to fortify Columbus Junction, Iowa.

(Bottom Left) The man-made levee temporarily holds back the rising water.

(Bottom Right). Workers assess the rising water and hope that the levee holds. It doesn't.

Joseph L. Murphy/IFBF

The levee breaches in Columbus Junction were repeated over the weekend in Oakville and Wapello, causing a rapid rise in the Iowa River. Another bout of storms in the region did not help matters.

The crest at Wapello of 32.15 feet was more than 2.5 feet above the 1993 record — but it could have been much worse in the city. That's because the river filled backwater areas, diffusing the water away from the river channel. Officials with the National Weather Service had feared the river would have exceeded 36 feet in the town.

As it was, the river crested more than a dozen feet above flood stage. And Oakville was next in line.

The town of 440 was hard hit by the flood. Every building in town was affected — homes, businesses, community centers — everything.

A year later, the recovery in Oakville is slow. More than 50 homes are now set to be destroyed, at a cost of $1.6 million. Another two dozen are yet to be repaired. Only 15 families have moved back into their homes, less than ten percent of those who called Oakville home before the flood.

But officials call it steady progress. Just like the 2009 Earth Day River Cleanup, where volunteers from around the country filled canoes and boats with trash in the first major cleanup of the Iowa near Oakville since the flood. At least three cabins had washed down the river, with the contents of each spilling out and washing up on the river bank. As a result of the volunteer activity, three tons of trash and debris were sent to the county landfill — appliances, furniture, and even clothing.

The devastation came in a single day, but it will take much longer than that to put Oakville back together.

By the time the Iowa emptied into the Mississippi at Burlington, the level barely exceeded that of 1993 — still a record, still 11 feet above flood stage.

The threat caused by the river during that devastating, staggering One Week in June came to an end in Iowa. But recovery was just beginning.

Opposite: The city of Oakville, Iowa was inundated with flood water after waters from the Iowa River broke a levee and spilled into town.

Jim Slosiarek/The Gazette

The Long Way Back

Liz Martin/The Gazette

This book has told just a part of the story of One Week in June — the amazing time in 2008 when record flooding and devastation struck our state, from its northern border to its southeastern edge. Each place the Cedar River went, it smashed records, and with them, thousands of lives — sometimes cresting twice in a single week. When the Cedar joined the swollen Iowa, its fury was only magnified.

Nature cannot really be contained, and our attempts to do so often only complicate matters. "Controlling" water flow one place, whether through permanent dams or temporary sandbag walls, only pushes the water into another place. Saving one part of a city, for example, may cause neighbors elsewhere in town to suffer more; just like keeping water away from "developed" areas may cause farm fields to flood more than they otherwise would.

In 2008, some cities bypassed their sewer directly into the river to keep sewage from backing up into people's homes. That made the river waters themselves even more poisoned than would otherwise have been the case. Output from city storm sewers that typically emptied into the river was blocked given the high river levels, leading to impromptu water fountains springing from manholes in streets — and water filling homes and businesses as a result.

Whatever goes into a river has to wind up somewhere, only adding to the volume carried downstream, raising the water level even more. It also adds to the cleanup task as the waters recede later.

And while attention was rightly focused on the progression of the Cedar downstream, day by day, it was hardly the only river that impacted Iowans that year.

Just as the Cedar crested in Charles City and Nashua, the Upper Iowa River breached a levee built by Luther College and broke a river record in Decorah that had stood since before World War II. The worst flooding in nearly 70 years struck the lower campus of the college, thanks to nine inches of rain falling in a 48-hour period onto already-saturated ground. The Upper Iowa crested on June 9 at 17.9 feet, 2.7 feet above the 1941 record. Nursing homes were evacuated, the town was split into two by the river, and — since the town's

Above: Josh Clemann (center) hands a box down to Justin Danford while Clemann's wife Jennifer Clemann watches from the second story window as the three clean the second story of the Clemanns' Time Check neighborhood home in northwest Cedar Rapids on Friday, June 20, 2008. They used the ladder to make the cleaning process easier than going through the house for each load.

Opposite: Recovery Construction Services workers Scott Yanda and Jeff Middleton, both of Cedar Rapids, haul damaged appliances out of Smulekoff's main store along the Cedar River on Friday, June 20, 2008, in southeast Cedar Rapids.

Iowa DOT trucks dump flood-damaged items at the Cedar Rapids/Linn County Solid Waste Agency facility at 2250 A St. SW in Cedar Rapids on Saturday, June 21, 2008.

three bridges spanning the Upper Iowa were closed — a nearly 90-mile-long detour, into Minnesota and back, was needed just to get from one side of Decorah to the other.

Elkader, along the Turkey River, suffered a reported $8 million of damage, with 20 homes completely destroyed and another nine suffering major damage; the waters rushing along Main Street soaked some 15 businesses. Officially, according to the National Weather Service, the 2008 record crest of 27.77 feet on June 10 was half a foot above the previous record, set in 1991, and 15 feet above flood stage. But most reports showed the river climbing to just under 31 feet in some areas of Elkader as water broke through a sandbag wall. Debris from a softball field, including a large light pole, passed over the city's dam end-over-end, and ultimately smashed into the back of the library. With Iowa Highway 13 closed, the city for a time permitted only emergency traffic. Citizens were forced to boil water as a precaution.

Jonathan D. Woods/The Gazette

Downtown Manchester flooded not once, not twice — but a total of four times in the summer of 2008 alone, thanks to the Maquoketa River. And those four crests, all among the top five of all time, came within six weeks. The last, on June 9, was 20.5 feet.

Not to be excluded, the Wapsipinicon River left its mark on Iowa communities as well. After setting one of the all-time marks in late April, the river again struck Independence, cresting at 18.86 feet on June 11, nearly seven feet above flood stage and leaving the fourth highest water mark in the history of the town.

Meanwhile, down river, the Wapsi's force and overflow from a rain-swollen Buffalo Creek led to a levee breach in Anamosa. Staff and inmates from the Iowa State Penitentiary joined volunteers who tried to sandbag around the city's waste water treatment facility. A concrete wall around the structure was designed to withstand a 100-year flood; even with sandbags, it was not enough this time, and efforts to save the plant were ultimately abandoned as the water

Clockwise:
Rockwell Collins employees volunteering with Serve The City, Victor Hu (second from left), Neil Rud and Bret Frieden scrape glued carpet up from the floor of the Salem Lighthouse youth center at Salem United Methodist Church in Cedar Rapids on Thursday, June 26, 2008.

A worker takes a break in an interior hallway at Theatre Cedar Rapids.

Bill Duffy of Cedar Rapids carries flood-damaged belongings from the home of John Arnold on Saturday, July 12, 2008, in southwest Cedar Rapids. Arnold lived in the home with his wife Joyce and their daughter Melinda.

Ginny Parrish photographs mold growing under the cabinets in the kitchen of her flood-damaged home along Edgewater Drive in Coralville on Tuesday, July 8, 2008.

Workers from Cotton National Disaster Recovery Company wash flood soiled windows in the Art Building West on the University of Iowa campus in Iowa City on Tuesday, July 8, 2008.

Liz Lillios (right) of Ambridge, Pennsylvania scoops debris up off the floor of Karen Hobert's home on 8th Avenue in southwest Cedar Rapids on Wednesday, June 25, 2008.

Chris Stumpff (left) of Cedar Rapids, and Clint Mersch of Swisher carry a water heater from the home of Dorothy Martens during flood cleanup on Hamilton Street SW.

Volunteer John Tenhundfeld (right) of Cedar Rapids takes a break from cleaning up flood damaged homes with District 5 councilman Justin Shields (left) in the parking lot of Westdale Mall on Saturday, June 28, 2008.

Theatre Cedar Rapids

Jim Slosiarek/The Gazette

Brian Ray/The Gazette

Brian Ray/The Gazette

Brian Ray/The Gazette

swiftly rose. Anamosa set records for river levels four times in 2008, including one in late March during the winter thaw. The all-time record, besting the old mark by 3.5 feet, was set on June 13 at 26.18 feet, more than a dozen feet above flood stage.

By the time the Wapsi hit DeWitt a second time in 2008, at more than three feet above flood stage over Father's Day weekend, it tied a record that had stood for nearly two decades.

In Iowa's capital city of Des Moines, the scene was eerily reminiscent of the record floods of 1993, when the city lost its water plant — and therefore, potable water — for weeks. On June 10, sandbaggers furiously began work to hold back the Raccoon River, which had devastated the city nearly 15 years before. It ultimately crested on June 13, two feet below the record mark, but still nearly double the level at flood stage. Water had filled ditches on each side of Interstate 80, leading to fears that the major roadway would have to be blocked north of the city. More water on both the Des Moines and Raccoon Rivers, and minor levee breaches, led to voluntary evacuations of parts of Des Moines over Father's Day weekend. The Des Moines River set new records at three metro-area reporting stations.

Iowa City's flooding was a product of the mighty Iowa River, which had made its presence known upstream during this One Week in June.

Marshalltown saw no fewer than three record crests in two weeks, each one worse than the one before. Ultimately, the high water mark there was 21.49 feet on June 13, more than a foot above the 1993 level, which had been the highest on record until the summer of 2008. The Tama County town of Chelsea was evacuated on June 11. In Marengo, the 1993 record

was bested by a foot, cresting at 21.23 feet on June 12. Officials there credited a strong levee system for keeping the situation from being even worse in town, but the water was therefore diverted into farm fields and parks, which were completely underwater, and roads around town were closed for a time.

The oldest record to fall during One Week in June was tied to the Shell Rock River, in its namesake town. Part of Iowa Highway 3 was swept away west of Shell Rock and the roadway was closed for weeks. In town, waters rose to completely cover street signs in many places. The river crested at 20.7 feet on June 10, 2.3 feet above the previous record level set in 1856.

The Shell Rock River left its mark elsewhere along the way. More than 400 homes in Rockford were affected when the crest came there on June 8, while part of the levee in Nora Springs was breached, leading to flooding there.

By the time the town of Greene saw the worst of the Shell Rock on June 9, two feet of standing water covered the town's Main Street business district, and a third of the town's citizens were in a shelter in the local high school. Ironically, Greene was to celebrate "River Days" the next weekend; the event was postponed.

Residents of Clarksville were surprised by the flooding, since the town had never before been affected by the force of the Shell Rock River. But when a railroad bed serving as a dike gave way overnight on June 9, a third of the town was saturated by rushing river water, reaching up to seven feet in some homes.

But perhaps most heartbreaking was what the 659 citizens of the Butler County town of New Hartford endured.

Brian Ray/The Gazette

Above: (from right) Tim Davin of Iowa City, Andy Hodge of Iowa City, and Kevin Harp of Iowa City toss sandbags in the bucket of a front end loader as they try to reopen the underground parking garage at the River Bend building on Wednesday, June 18, 2008 in Coralville.

Opposite: Cleaning up after the flood primarily on the Arts Campus.

Courtney Sargent/The Gazette

Left: Major Brian Gardner (left) of the Linn County Sheriff Department and Linda Langston of the Linn County Board of Supervisors get a tour of the flood damaged basement of the Linn County Jail in Cedar Rapids on Thursday, July 3, 2008.

Opposite (Clockwise): Several messages have sprung up on homes and businesses impacted by flooding, like this one at Skinflix Custom Ink, 227 14th Ave. SE, on Monday, July 14, 2008.

Volunteer Candace Chihak (left) of Lisbon breaks through the wall of Gloria Ruzicka's kitchen as other volunteers help to remove the flood-damaged drywall in southwest Cedar Rapids on Saturday, June 28, 2008.

Hands On Disaster Response volunteer Jeremy Horan of Aspen, Colorado installs drywall in Rich and Faye Dykema's basement, which was filled with four feet of flood water in Palo, on Tuesday, July 22, 2008.

Westside Maid-Rite owner Jim Hanson (right) discusses the trim he and his son Jason Hanson of Prairieburg (left) are installing around the windows of the restaurant on Tuesday, July 15, 2008 in Cedar Rapids. The Hansons were working to get the business open by the next week.

A message to neighbors from a homeowner on Fourth Street and L Ave. NW in the Time Check neighborhood.

Only two weeks after a historic EF-5 tornado devastated New Hartford and Parkersburg, Beaver Creek spilled over a dike on the west side of town. After one of the wettest seasons on record, the creek was already full when even more early June rain caused it to rush into town. Virtually every home in town was affected by flooding, and the whole town was urged to leave on June 9.

Simply put, officials said that what wasn't affected by the tornado was hit by the flood.

The sheer numbers from the flooding are staggering. As a result of the 2008 early summer weather, Iowa Governor Chet Culver declared 86 of Iowa's 99 counties disaster areas. That translates to 45,000 out of Iowa's 56,272 square miles, encompassing 700 of the 947 cities and towns in the state.

According to the Rebuild Iowa Office (RIO), established by the state in response to the Iowa Floods of 2008, 38,000 people were displaced by tornadoes and flooding.

Above and Opposite:
The flood couldn't wash
away American pride
in the Time Check
neighborhood.

From north to south, an estimated six million sandbags were used, with one million of those in the Iowa City/Coralville area alone.

Iowa's roads and highways sustained $30 million of damage. More than 450 miles of road and 300 bridges/culverts were closed.

The effects on agriculture were difficult to measure, but 1.2 million acres of corn and soybeans were lost due to the June flooding. Many of those fields were barely planted, due to the already-wet spring. While some areas were replanted later and did yield crops, the agricultural damages from the eastern Iowa 2008 flooding were 2.5 to 3 times greater than during the 2003 floods statewide.

The havoc wreaked by the flooding was made worse by the fact that Iowa endured a record-setting 15-day wet period during the first half of June 2008, including the record-setting One Week in June. This damp spell closely followed the month of April, which was the second-wettest April in history.

When you then consider that the preceding winter (2007-2008) was the eighth wettest on record, and the year before the great floods, 2007, was the fourth wettest in 135 years of recordkeeping…in hindsight, it's not surprising that it all happened as it did.

It was the perfect set of factors, aligned in a way to show us who was really in charge.

But those are just numbers and statistics. What was really memorable was how Iowans responded to the challenges with the spirit that we always call upon in such times.

More than one service agency noted that they actually had a hard time getting citizens to accept help in cleaning out their flood-ravaged homes. "Thanks,

but I've got it covered," Mr. Jacobs would say. "You should go help out my neighbors, the Brown family. They've really got it bad."

When the volunteers arrived at the Brown house, Mrs. Brown would politely decline the help.
"I think we can handle it," she'd say. "But if you want to help someone, go over to the Jacobs place. I really feel for them."

And after a while, we might grudgingly accept some help, even if it came from unlikely sources. The city of Waverly, settled 150 years ago with a strong German heritage, saw volunteers from the Jewish-based volunteer group Nechama (the Hebrew word for "comfort") set up camp in town for weeks after the flood — no questions asked.

When a group of administration and staff members from Cornell College came to help a man who owned several rental properties affected by the flood in Cedar Rapids, the man had his wife bring their young grandchildren to the site later in the day to introduce them to the people who had donated their time to help someone they didn't even know. "This is what you do," he told them, as he had them shake hands with each of the volunteers. "You help people when they need help."

Iowans extended their hands…not looking for a hand out, but ready to offer a helping hand to others even when they could have used help themselves. And they did it without complaining.

Mother Nature tested us during 2008, especially during that One Week in June. She may have left her mark — but we still won, as a people, as Iowans.

We always have. And if One Week in June was any indication, we always will.

About the Author

Jeff Stein is an educator, journalist and attorney. He holds the title of R.J. McElroy Chair and Executive-in-Residence in Communication Arts at Wartburg College, teaching broadcasting and media law and ethics courses. He is also the administrator of the Archives of Iowa Broadcasting collection and has spoken around the country on broadcasting, journalism, and mass media topics. Stein is the author of *Making Waves: The People and Places of Iowa Broadcasting* (WDG Publishing, 2004) and *Covering Iowa Law and Courts: A Guide for Journalists* (Iowa State Bar Association, 1996, 2001). He is the 2009 recipient of the Jack Shelley Award, the highest honor presented to Iowa broadcast journalists, from the Iowa Broadcast News Association.